2011
THE BEST WOMEN'S
MONOLOGUES AND SCENES

2011
THE BEST WOMEN'S
MONOLOGUES AND SCENES

Edited and with a Foreword
by Lawrence Harbison

MONOLOGUE AUDITION SERIES

SMITH AND KRAUS PUBLISHERS
177 LYME ROAD, HANOVER, NH 03755
EDITORIAL 603.643.6431 TO ORDER 1800.558.2846
www.smithandkraus.com

A Smith and Kraus Book
Published by Smith and Kraus, Inc.
177 Lyme Road, Hanover, NH 03755
www.SmithandKraus.com

First Edition: March 2012
10 9 8 7 6 5 4 3 2 1

Manufactured in the United States of America
Cover design by Emily Kent, emilygkent@gmail.com
Book design by Nathan Spring, nespring@gmail.com

ISBN-10 1-57525-781-5 ISBN-13 978-1-57525-781-5 ISSN 2164-2362

CONTENTS

SCENES

FOREWORD

Here you will find a rich and varied selection of monologues and scenes from plays which were produced and/or published in the 2010-2011 theatrical season. Most are for younger performers (teens through 30s) but there are also some excellent pieces for women in their 40s and 50s, and even a few for older performers. Some are comic (laughs), some are dramatic (generally, no laughs). Some are rather short, some are rather long. All represent the best in contemporary playwriting.

Several of the monologues are by playwrights whose work may be familiar to you such as Don Nigro, Stephen Belber, Charles Busch, Donald Margulies and Naomi Wallace; others are by exciting up-and-comers such as Nicole Pandolfo, Leslye Headland, Tracey Thorne, Kim Rosenstock, Zoe Kazan, Samuel D. Hunter, Allison Moore, Lauren Yee and Steven Levenson The scenes are mostly by exciting new writers, such as Alexander Dinaris, Deirdre O'Connor and Molly Smith Metzler. All are representative of the best of contemporary writing for the stage.

Most of the plays from which these monologues have been culled have been published and, hence, are readily available either from the publisher/licensor or from a theatrical book store such as Drama Book Shop in New York. A few plays may not be published for a while, in which case contact the author or his agent to request a copy of the entire text of the play, which contains the monologue which suits your fancy. Information on publishers/rights holders may be found in the Rights & Permissions section in the back of this anthology.

Break a leg in that audition! Knock 'em dead in class!

Lawrence Harbison
Brooklyn, New York

MONOLOGUES

Afterlife: A Ghost Story

Steve Yockey

Dramatic
Danielle, 30s

> *Danielle is sitting outside, staring at the ocean. She has recently lost her son and here she expresses her feelings about this, sort of to God.*

DANIELLE: You're not fooling anyone, you know? Well, you're not fooling me. You're a false neighbor. Maybe something I should have expected. Am I naïve? To be fair, I 'm not fooling anyone either. I wasn't fooling anyone, but the secret is really out now. Connor's packing the car. I should be trying to help, trying to talk to him. Trying to apologize. Jesus, we never even put up the storm shutters. Huh, but instead of anywhere else, here I am. And just look at me. And just look at you. You know, since you took our son, my son, I think my heart actually pumps slower. Like it takes more for it to keep going. Like I have to really try when it used to be so effortless. Honestly, it feels like it would be easier to just give in than keep overcoming the pain of every beat, every beat that sends blood rushing out to find, when it reaches my eyes, my hands in this fucking sand, that I'm still alone. Even with Connor, I'm alone. All I have here are memories that I can't enjoy ever again and you: a vast, never-ending gravesite. Aren't you pretty? But we're not so different, you and me. Wave after wave after wave thrown against the shore, the same motion over and over again, clawing at the beach like each time you might get a solid grip. And instead, slowly over time, you just drag everything away. Out there. In here.
> *(She points to her head.)*
And in here.
> *(She touches her chest.)*
I do that too, the same feelings, the same thoughts, over and over. I want him back. I hate you. I want him back. I hate you. You think maybe we do it because we don't know how to do anything else, like something inside is truly broken but keeps trying to finish anyway? Honestly, it's not just you and me though, I guess. There's Connor, poor well- meaning, "recovering" Connor. That's not fair. And there's all of our family who don't know me anymore, how could they know me? They can't see me anymore. I can't see me anymore. All I can see is you. And I do see you. I

fucking see you now, the real you, so hungry and large. How could I ever have trusted something that does nothing but take? Do you have him out there somewhere? Holding him tight so he can't come home. I should let you take me, too. Would you like that? Do you want that? Let you reach in through my mouth and pull everything out it one motion so I just buckle and collapse, my lungs, my heart, all of it. I would give you all of it if you'd just take these memories, too.

(She stands up.)

We lived next to you for years and you just couldn't resist, could you? He was a beautiful boy and you wanted him. So you took him because you get what you want, right? You're a beast. And I do hate you. I hate you. I hate you! I hate...

(Lightning crashes causing Danielle to leap a bit.)

Fucking ocean.

Alive and Well

Kenny Finkle

Seriocomic
Carla Keenan, 30's

> *Carla, a newly unemployed and single New York City journalist, has taken a mysterious, well paying job in Virginia looking for The Lonesome Soldier, a Confederate Soldier who has been making appearances around the state. her guide Zach is proving every bit as annoying as the miles of tramping lost through the woods with no cell reception and getting caught in a torrential downpour. Now having found respite in an old cabin and a flask of whiskey she drops her tough as nails demeanor to reveal to Zach what brought her to this place in her life.*

CARLA: You offend me, you know that? How can you not like marshmallows? Marshmallows are delicious. When I was eight I ate marshmallows for seven days straight once. I love marshmallows. Marshmallows, marshmallows, marshmallows, mershmallllsss… My grandmother loved marshmallows too.

She taught me about art. My grandmother did. She used to take me to museums every Saturday when I was growing up and we'd look at art together. And she was an artist too. She wouldn't have called herself that though, she would have called herself a housewife. But she did make art Mr. Clemenson. Beautiful art. She had this one piece, I don't know how to explain it, its just a piece of marble that she shaped in two concentric pieces but one of the sides comes to a point, and out of it there's a break in the marble, a different color, a red, that makes a line down to the bottom of the piece, a little crack of red in the grey. And it makes me feel so much pain. And I don't know why. I want to know why it makes me feel. She just died. She was the most important person in my life. I'd talk to her about everything and now I have no one to talk to about anything. I'm lost without her. I don't know who I am or what I'm supposed to be doing anymore. I don't know right from wrong. I've lost my moral compass. I've lost my way. What am I saying? Mr. Clemenson I do believe this whiskey has gone straight to my head.

Alive and Well

Kenny Finkle

Seriocomic
Carla Keenan, 30's

> *Carla, a newly unemployed and single New York City journalist, has taken
> a mysterious, well paying job in Virginia looking for The Lonesome Soldier,
> a Confederate Soldier who has been making appearances around the state.
> her guide Zach is proving every bit as annoying as the miles of tramping lost
> through the woods with no cell reception and getting caught in a torrential
> downpour. Now having found respite in an old cabin and a flask of whiskey
> she drops her tough as nails demeanor to reveal to Zach what brought her to
> this place in her life.*

CARLA: My fiance'. Ex fiancé. He just left me. Screw you Lou! I hate Lou.
That's not true. Lou says I have a compulsive need to tell the truth all
the time. He says when I lie, even the littlest lie it seems to haunt me,
like the tell tale heart and then I have to confess. And it's true I do
and Mr. Clemenson, I've been haunted for days now because I have a
lot to confess to you. Mr. Clemenson I'm here under somewhat false
pretenses… I don't know who I'm working for… I got this job from an ad
on Craigslist! I took the job for the money. Five thousand dollars! That's
how much I'm getting paid! The ad said they were a major magazine and
they sent me half my fee and I'm supposed to get the rest when I turn
in the story and 2500 dollars is a lot of money for me right now because
I can't pay my rent because Lou left me and my credit cards are maxed
and I used to write for a newspaper but newspapers are dying and so I
was fired and I can't seem to get another job and I've won awards! But
no one cares. That's not true, people care but not enough people so I was
cut. And that made me angry. That's not true, I was angry before that.
That's not true, I wasn't angry, I was misunderstood and that makes me
angry because no one understands me. Not even Lou. When we were at
the Virginia Diner, that was him that texted me. He was in the apartment
getting his stuff and he wanted to know who should get the Joni Mitchell
cds. "I get the Joni Mitchell cds dillweed I get them!!" Which is what I
texted him. He should have known that! Why didn't he know that? He
should have known that I love Joni Mitchell! Joni Mitchell tells the truth!
Joni Mitchell is my idol! I wish I were Joni Mitchell singing the truth at

the top of my lungs –

All in the Faculty

William Fowkes

Comic
Marlene, early 30s

> *Marlene Bernstein, a professor of French, finds the lack of social and marital prospects in a small college town demoralizing. her strategy for coping is to scour each year's crop of new single faculty members hoping to find the possibility of love. When she meets Ned Jenkins, she thinks her search is over, but soon becomes disillusioned with their on-again-off-again relationship. Three years later, Ned is about to leave academia and Marlene behind, and she feels compelled to stop by to take one more shot at making him understand what went wrong; or is it one more shot at love?*

MARLENE: That's exactly why left you.

You were never fully there for me. And I never understood why. I thought maybe you had some sort of interpersonal attention deficit disorder. Like your obsession with movies – watching them over and over again. I can't watch the same movie twenty-three times. I thought I must not be as deep as you … But I don't think that's it at all! I think I see everything the first time through. I think I GET it. Just as I think I get YOU. I think I KNOW you; but I don't think you know ME. I think you like to watch the same movies over and over, because you're never fully there the first time around. You're like people on marijuana. They think they're brilliant, but they're not even here - they're just fucked up. And YOU'RE fucked up! That's it, isn't it - that's got to be the explanation!

(She stands up abruptly.)

You're fucked up! … Why? Why are you fucked up? It's not fair! Why should I fall in love with someone who's fucked up?

(She laughs and/or cries and then stops herself)

Oh, mon dieu! Pardonnez-moi, monsieur! *(After a pause.)* I must be the one who's fucked up. I don't even like the "f" word, and right now it's the only thing I feel like saying.

(Calming down.)

Of course, you'll be a gentleman and forget this ever happened. We don't need to part like this.

No, please don't touch me

Don't listen to me, Ned! Hold me!

The Awakening of Kate Chopin

Rosary O'Neill

Dramatic
Kate Chopin, 32

> *Kate, an educated high achiever and Irish beauty, is married to Oscar, 39, a tyrannical cotton merchant. Bankrupt, they have retreated to her in-laws in Cloutierville, Louisiana, a one-street town blighted by the Civil War. Kate confronts Oscar's threat to burn her manuscript of her novel The Awakening.*

KATE: I feel compelled to tell my truth regardless of …You think it's easy to close myself off. I've got to believe my story matters, because only I can tell it from a place of absolute passion. I can't worry about being . . . sued and lynched. I have a right to express myself regardless- I'm trying to speak from gentleness. I don't want to be vengeful. I WANT to write from a place that invites people in. But I don't feel like most women. I have to find that stance-the grace, balancing. Personally I'm not gracious. The first time around. It takes drafts for me to get to kindness. It's true I'm interested in a thoughtful look at relationships. Maybe if you could find the brokenness in yourself, you could understand my dark side. I understand women have limited choices. But at what point do I stop making excuses for-- It's not a woman's concern. I want to be free to be angry, to thrash around in the gore and still be a woman. I WON'T rewrite this. . . .Change myself and this material- Threaten me once more, and I'll leave you for dead.

Birthday
Crystal Skillman

Comic
Leila, 29

Leila, dragged to a bar to celebrate a co-workers birthday, bursts into what she thinks is an empty room, crying (we discover later in the play it is actually her birthday, which no one knows); but there she finds a man in his early thirties, Kyle, a seemingly well off, all together, quiet kind of guy listening to his i-pod. Leila, avoiding returning to the party in the next room, desperately seeking some kind of connection, finds her babbly, awkward self opening up to this stranger.

LEILA: You like your stout. I never know what to get here - I just got mine because of the name. Old Speckled Hen. I think because I'm obsessed with farms. All that driving through fields and passing barns all the time when I was a kid. I did 4 H and all that, and I was, I was shit at it. Animals kinda hate me actually, I think. I was like in high school coming back from some Thanksgiving thing with my parents - and there was this horse in the middle of the road. No one else around. And instead of, I don't know calling someone, my mom gets like "We've got to help it." This horse is like a baby elephant. Huge to me. Somehow my mom's shrill voice (which would probably make me run into ongoing traffic) seems to be coxing the horse over to the park. I'm just following behind, my head low like please God don't let anybody see my stupid ass mom talking to a horse on Sheafe Road. But we do get him off the road. It's like a miracle. It worked. And then I'm like, you know I feel something for this horse we saved, his eyes are like gleaming and it seems like there's a connection, you know? And I want to touch him. I take like one step and he rears up. It's like unreal - the setting sun behind blinding off the snow and thank god I totally remembered how in *Gandhi* Ben Kinsley threw his boney ass to the ground to save everyone from these charging horses. And it works – the horse settles, trots toward the barn. When we get home and I go the bathroom and I don't know how but somehow when it raised up, the horse totally grazed me and so there's like a cut on ...

(motions to her breast)

I mean I'm like, kill me now. I tell my mom and then she's calling the doctor and like, "Yes, I know it's Thanksgiving but I'm calling because my daughter got bitten on her breast by a horse." And later I thought, of course this happened. Because any time you try too hard. Reach out. Help. This is what happens. You get – classic tit chomping horse stories. Christ - do you know that I recount my life to homeless people on the street. I go to the tops of towers and scream out my life. MTA guys. Waitresses. Cab drivers, they try to tell me their shit but I cut them off and tell them what happened to me. Fuck ...I'm going to shut up. I'm shutting up now.

(Beat.)

I should. I really should –

The Break of Noon

Neil LaBute

Ginger, 30s-40s

> *Ginger's ex-husband has recently had a brush with death. A madman came into where he worked and shot and killed everyone but him. During the shooting spree, he heard the voice of God, telling him he would be saved. He has decided to make amends to those he has hurt in his life, and has asked Ginger for forgiveness. She thinks he's crazy and, anyway, it's too late for forgiveness.*

GINGER: I'm taking the car, John. I need to get back to, you know...the real world. To Civilization. Earth.

    (Beat.)

You scare me now--worse than ever before. I wish you were a serial killer. I do. That you'd been found to be living some double life with girls chained up in a basement. Or a war criminal--I don't care how many women you'd raped or children or Jews that you might've killed...any of that shit would be easier to understand than this. And I mean that, as nutty as it sounds.

    (Beat.)

God doesn't mean anything to us anymore. He's the boogyman, that's all. Someone that parents use to scare their children into doing what they want 'em to do. It's the truth, John--it's not comforting, I'm not happy when you say this shit to me... when we die, we die. That's it. No Jesus, no Heaven. It's bullshit and I knew it at six. We do what we do, we make choices and we're responsible--you were a shitty husband and now you're sorry. Some man, he put a gun in your face and you're feeling bad about your life and you wanna change it. Fine. Do something. Change how you live the rest of it but that doesn't mean God is divine and he spoke to you... that is a crock of shit and you know it! In your heart? You know that...just be a man and say so. Go out and spread the gospel of "I used to be a motherfucking asshole." Try that. Or ask my forgiveness for how you treated me and we'll be even.

    (Beat.)

I don't need the money. I do not need all this crap you're doing here. No, I don't. An apology would be enough...

A Bright New Boise
Samuel D. Hunter

Dramatic
Pauline, late 30s-early 40s

Pauline, a manager at a Hobby Lobby in Boise, Idaho, has just learned that one of her employees has a few skeletons in his closet that May damage the reputation of her store if the public were to find out. Here, Pauline tries to make this employee understand exactly what the Hobby Lobby means to her.

PAULINE: I'm gonna say this once, and I hope you understand me. *(Pause.)* I took over this store four years ago. The first day I was here, four out of six cashiers called in sick, there were rats in the stock room, and a good quarter of all items on the floor were mis-stocked or mis-labeled. The manager before me, this little pip-squeak from Nampa, he saw there was mold problem in the air ducts so his solution was to puncture an air freshener and toss it inside. It was chaos, you understand? Corporate told me I was taking over as a temporary measure, to oversee the branch for six months before, they said, they would most likely close it completely. And what did I do? I cleaned it up. I stayed here during nights by myself restocking and organizing, cleaning the air ducts, firing and hiring and basically reshaping this entire store from the ground up. I took out ads in the paper announcing new management and grand-reopening sales. Six months later, our profits were up sixty-two percent, and they've been climbing ever since. I, Will, I brought order to chaos. Goddam right it's impressive. Damn near miraculous. And it happened because of me. Because I changed everything about this store, I changed the way this store feels, the way it thinks, the fucking ecosystem in this store. And I will not have you or anyone else disrupting the ecosystem I have painstakingly crafted. *(Pause.)* Listen, personally, I don't give a shit what you believe. But as far as the good people of Boise are concerned, you are a state-wide embarrassment. And if people were to find out that one of our cashiers is from this wacky little cult up north, they may think about buying their silk flowers somewhere else. *(Pause.)* When you're in this store, just—stay away from Alex, understand? And I don't want anyone else finding out about this church of yours. No customers, no co-workers, no one. *(Pause.)* You're on register four.

Class

Charles Evered

Dramatic
Sarah, early 20's.

Sarah, a movie star, is explaining to Elliot, her acting teacher in New York, how she first learned she was dying.

SARAH: Well, I wasn't feeling well, you know, for the longest time, and I had some suspicions about some things, and I went on the internet to try to find out what I was dying of, because I just assumed I was dying, I always assumed I was, whenever there was anything the least bit---whenever something was out of the ordinary, and the internet is the totally worst place to go because there's just so much information that no matter what symptom you write in, lists of like eighty thousand things you could be dying of come up and you just can't go that route or it will drive you absolutely crazy, so I went to a doctor I know in LA at Cedars, and he started this whole battery of tests and at first everything checked out, and I was kind of feeling really good about things and then one morning, when I was baking a batch of whole grain muffins--the phone rang. It's so funny how things freeze in your head, but I remember looking at the phone ringing, and it had rung about 3 times before I picked it up and when I put it to my ear, it was from *that* very instant that everything went into this sort of slow motion dance --and I knew right away what he was going to tell me. "Sarah?" he said, in this super empathetic "I'm about to tell you you're dying voice," "Sarah, this is Dr. Yoblinsky. I'm afraid I have some…" *(pause)* And then ya know what? My first thought was: "Wow, when I put these muffins in the oven I didn't know I was dying, and when I took them out---." And I thought, "Gee whiz, isn't life funny that way? But ya know, Elliot, in some ways I was totally relieved. For the first time in my life I wouldn't have to worry about whether I was dying or not. Crazy, I know, but then---I sort of am. So I hung up the phone with Dr. Yoblinsky, walked into my bedroom, closed the door, pulled down all the shades and sat in the middle of my bed for 16 hours straight. Not crying, not spazzing out, nothing, just sitting there, playing a black and white movie of my entire life in my head: every crossroad, all the wonderful things, all the bad, isolating every little instant where I made a choice that led me down some road, which then led me down some other road where I would be forced to make a choice that would lead me down some other road---and all this time, Elliot, there in the dark, that's all I did. Tracing my entire life like that---all the way back from when I could actually remember remembering. When I got out of bed I walked into my kitchen and saw my cell phone on the floor. Apparently it had vibrated so much it vibrated itself right off the kitchen counter and onto my brand new Italian hand crafted tile floor. And there it was, spinning and dancing and vibrating all over my one hundred and fourteen thousand dollar floor and so I picked it up, checked it, and I had sixty seven new voicemails. Twenty eight of them were from my manager, freaked that I had missed some sort of photo shoot or something, fifteen were from my agent, eleven were from my publicist, seven were from my stylist, five were from a car service and one was an automated message from the Census Bureau. After I hung up the phone, I ran into my room again and rifled through one of my Kate Spades and found the little piece of paper my agent had written your name and number on. I booked a flight on my way to the airport and--- here I be.

Clytemnestra

Don Nigro

Dramatic
Carolyn Ryan, 46

In the bathroom of their house in Armitage, a small town in east Ohio, in the year 1919, Carolyn Ryan, 46, is speaking to her husband, Michael, who's taking a bath. Michael has just come home from the First World War, and is depressed and contemplating suicide. While he was gone, Carolyn had an affair with the husband of her daughter, Jenna, whom she'd managed to get committed to a mental institution. Now Carolyn wants to make her marriage work, but Michael won't sleep with her. He spends all his time in the study reading ancient Greek plays, or in the bath. Her growing frustration has been increased greatly by learning from her dying father, who's obsessed by squirrels, that her real father is the village idiot. She's been having terrible headaches and is getting more and more upset. She's longing desperately for her husband to love her again.

CAROLYN: We used to do it like dogs. Dogwise, on the roof, looking at the stars. When you were late, I kept a light burning in the window for you. I liked so much the way you kissed my knees. When I was taking a bath, you'd come in and kiss my knees. You haven't kissed my knees in a thousand years. *(Pause.)* What are you doing here? I mean, what are you doing here, in this house. What are you doing in this house? You don't live here. You haven't lived here for a long time, and even when you did live here you didn't live here. You were never really here. I don't know where you were, but it wasn't here. And then you left and now you're back but you aren't really. You never left because you never were here and you can't come back to a place you never were, but here you are and what the hell am I supposed to do with you? I'm making sandwiches for the village idiot and my head feels like it's going to explode and my father doesn't want any more squirrels and I don't know who I am or what the hell I'm supposed to do with you. I put the knife down and came up here to see you and when I got to the door I couldn't come in. I was afraid to come in. I was afraid to see my own husband. So I went down to your study and sat there reading your English translation of Aeschylus, in a desperate attempt to understand what the hell is going on inside your head. I'm forced to read a play written by a dead Greek four or five hundred years before Christ to understand the man who put three children inside me. And the only completely frank and honest conversation I've had in years was with the village idiot, who screwed my mother in the cemetery, and I think my head is going to explode.

Clytemnestra

Don Nigro

Dramatic
Carolyn Ryan, 46

In the bathroom of their house in Armitage, Ohio, Carolyn Ryan is in the midst of an increasingly violent argument with her husband, Michael, who's home from the First World War, and now spends nearly all his time reading Greek tragedies or taking long baths, as he is now. Carolyn has betrayed him with her daughter's husband while Michael was away, but now wants desperately to get Michael's love again. She's even been reading his Greek plays to try and connect with him. But Michael has just admitted to her that he met an English nurse in the war, a woman he could actually talk to. He has always had problems communicating with the volatile and impatient Carolyn. Michael has a pair of scissors his daughter was cutting his hair with and the possibility of suicide has crossed his mind. Michael is in fact a Greek immigrant from New York who fled to Ohio after murdering an old man and stealing his money. He took the name Ryan from a dead man on a train. His whole life has been a lie. He's just told her he doesn't want anything from her. He thinks the only answer for him is to give up everything, but he doesn't think she can possibly understand. She is very frustrated, upset and angry, and is just about at the end of her rope.

CAROLYN: No. I understand. And I think I can help you with that. I mean with giving up everything. Doesn't his wife murder him in his bath? He comes home from the Trojan War. His wife murders him in his bath. Clytemnestra. That's her name. She's taken a lover and he's taken a lover and she's furious with him and she solves her problem by stabbing him to death in the bath. Is that why you come home and sit there in the bath tub all night and tell me this? So I'll kill you? Because I've been reading this stupid thing, and I think I'm finally beginning to understand what you mean about myths recurring over and over again. You love the Greeks. You identify with the Greeks. You are a Greek. You're not a Ryan. You're a—what the hell was your name, anyway? And you've made us all Greeks. You've turned your whole family into some sort of a goddamned Greek tragedy, and now we're trapped, like flies in a web, and we can't get out. You'd have killed yourself a long time ago but you want me to do it so your children can have the insurance money. Well, I don't give a damn about the insurance money, and I don't give a damn about your children, either. I just want out. But there's no way out. Let me out. Why don't you just take those damned scissors and stick them in your chest. Go on. See if I care. See if I care about your damned insurance money. You can die in the bath like stupid fucking what's his name.

Collapse

Allison Moore

Seriocomic
Hannah, mid-30s

Hannah is trying to explain to the nice older man who has just busted her for eavesdropping on a 12-step meeting in a church basement that she was not, in fact, eavesdropping. Hannah is a little high-strung.

HANNAH: I really wasn't trying to eavesdrop. I just, I got lost! I've never been here before, I mean, I'm not even here for me! My husband is the one who was supposed to come. He said he was going to, but then my sister showed up from California. She just showed up, and it looks like she's planning to, to, move in. And I love my sister, I do, but she can be a little much? And then David refused to come—not to AA, it's a different kind of support group. Not that there's anything wrong with AA! I think it's wonderful that you're an alcoholic! I mean, okay, that came out wrong. It's probably not wonderful, I'm just trying to say: AA is great, and if my husband were an alcoholic—which I don't think he is, I mean, I worry sometimes about his drinking? Because he's been drinking a lot lately? But the doctor said that's very common for people in his situation, it's like self-medication. But I really think the root of the problem is that he just needs to talk, to anyone, which is why I wanted him to come to this support group. I think it would help him so much, but then Susan showed up, and David wouldn't come, and now they're at home getting drunk and I'm here! And by the time I got here it was 8:30, and there were three different meetings going on, and one of them was definitely a group of lesbians so I knew that wasn't it. But I couldn't tell which of the other two was the right group. But I couldn't go home because then David would say, 'See? It was waste of time!' And then he'll never come! And if he doesn't come, if he doesn't get some kind of help, I don't know what I'm gonna do. I just, I can't take it anymore.

(Hannah is crying.)

So I stood in the hallway, lurking. I admit it. I lurked, I and I'm sorry for that. But I swear to you, I was not eavesdropping. I just, I don't know what to do anymore.

A Common Vision

Neena Beber

Dramatic
Dolores, 30s

Dolores believes she was abducted by aliens. here she talks to a skeptical friend about what that experience meant to her.

DOLORES: I know what you're thinking: why would she be chosen? Why would anyone find her special? Why her? It's not a question of "belief." Do you believe in trees? In sky, in milk, in the ocean? Do you believe that I'm sitting here talking to you now, do you believe what you see? Because I have witnesses. I was seen. What about light? What about air, the wind? What about the things you don't see? A feeling, maybe. A soul, maybe. Do you believe we have one? Do you know what it's like to spend your whole life in heartache? Always longing for something and not knowing why, this hole, and then... then...it's like a gift, really. You don't? You're just a speck. Like me. Insignificant. But maybe, maybe we're important; maybe there's a plan and I'm included. You don't know what it feels like, you can't say. Because you've probably always felt that you were important, that you counted, mattered, you've probably always. Felt that way.

A Confluence of Dreaming

Tammy Ryan

Comic
Morgan, 17

Morgan confronts her mother after discovering a sexy e-mail her mother has written to a man via the internet.

MORGAN: Mom, don't confuse reality with the internet. I know how tempting it is, because I been there done that already. Confused reality with the Land of Oz. It happens to everybody when they first get online. You're going along lahdeedah in your normal Kansean existence when out of nowhere this technology descends on you like a tornado. You get swept up in it and it takes you where IT wants to. Then before you know it, you find yourself in a strange place called a CHATROOM with all these wild characters and you keep getting drawn further in by the promise of what's down that yellow brick road. You're thinking this is great, I get to wear the magic ruby slippers and chat with all these cool people and you start to think, hey, this is where I can make all my dreams come true. Face it Mom, you're addicted. I don't blame you. Given the choice between Oz and Kansas who wouldn't take Oz. Oz is a colorful place inhabited by happy mindless munchkins where everybody sings and dances. There's a funny well meaning scarecrow, a harmless cowardly lion and a weepy tin man. Kansas is gray, boring, predictable, and the roof leaks. But there's also flying monkeys and violent trees and a wicked witch who would kill you as soon as look at you so you have to stay awake when you're crossing that field of poppies because not everything is what it seems. For one thing there's a nerdy guy behind the curtain, he's a geek, more than a little strange, and he's working his smoke and mirrors hoping you stay focused on the image he's projecting on the screen because he has absolutely no power. It's your willingness to be deceived by him that makes him powerful. Look behind the curtain. That's all I'm saying.

A Confluence of Dreaming

Tammy Ryan

Dramatic
Carol, 48

Carol, a wife and suburban stay-at-home mom, is talking to her daughter Morgan, 17. Carol has been having a cyber affair with a stranger she's met on the internet, and Morgan has discovered one of her e-mails to him. At this moment, mother and daughter are in the middle of an argument about whether or not Morgan is going to college.

CAROL: Every generation thinks it's going to change the world, you are not the first, but you'll grow up and you'll see it can't be done. The only thing you can do is take care of yourself, and that's what I'm trying to help you do. Go to college, get an education, get a job. Then you can do what you want-- But I can see already what's going to happen to you. Cause you won't think any more than I did. You'll meet some guy, fall in love and get married. And then everything you want now will go out the window. Because you'll have kids and you won't have time for any of this nonsense anymore. Because you'll be just like me, Morgan, living day to day: going shopping, cooking meals, yes, cleaning the house, doing the laundry, taking the cat to the vet, taking care of everyone else, and there won't be time for any other nonsense, like worrying about who we're bombing. Because we are always bombing someone! And what you have to do today nibbles and nibbles and nibbles away until there's nothing left. Your concept of the planet will shrink to the size of your kitchen island and humanity will be the people sitting around it who have hooked up their vacuum cleaners to your jugular and have sucked, sucked, sucked everything out until your soul has become as a dry as a desert.
(Carol bursts into tears.)
So don't talk to me about my soul.

The Death Bite

Hal Corley

Dramatic
Felicia, 15

Felicia was recently placed in her final foster home with Robyn, a loving but beleaguered working class single woman. When Robyn discovers Felicia has been stealing from her, she confronts her. Knowing she'll soon age out of the system and after years of foster drift end up homeless, Felicia makes a desperate last stand to stay with Robyn, incorrectly assuming that Robyn's feelings for her are more than maternal.

FELICIA: A mom? A mom's no better than anybody else. Look at yours. Or mine. 'Last time they let me see her? She blurts out how Jesus had appeared, and sat on her bed. Even if getting messed up on bad prison drugs made it happen, this wacko, figuring out she's, like, best friends with Jesus was supposed to matter? To me? And I'd already heard: she killed her own brother, and didn't even feel bad about it. Didn't even do it to defend herself. He just didn't cut her in her share of some money, so she grabbed his gun and shot him in the neck. When she was six months pregnant carryin' my half sister, who was already dead inside her. And I was peein' on myself in a cardboard box in the corner like one of your cats takin' a leak 'cause she never bought diapers. Right before, she'd been puttin' on nail polish, and got it all over the gun. Whatta idiot. Some lawyer the court stuck her with said it was all 'cause pregnant woman hormones made her do it. But that's so lame. It was just her. "Jesus sat on her bed." Right. Took her years to sign off on giving me up. Not 'cause she hated to let me go, but 'cause she thought holding off on the papers might get her out early. That's a mom for ya.

    (Beat.)

If you'd just forget all that, including stuff I did, and just said? Just now? And let me stay on? We could, like, fix stuff, you n' me. Start over. Maybe just be good friends this time? 'Whole mom and daughter thing didn't work. So? Didn't work anyplace else I lived. I could still be your "Cookie." Hey, like you said, I'm smart. I've noticed stuff. Like, how you sneak peeks. When I'm going back to my room? In a towel? I see you 'round Haidee, too. The way you take care of her? Wait on her? Yeah, right, I get what all that's about. You're a single lady with no men friends. Who just decides one day to go adopt some teenage girl? Who 'you kidding? You don't have to pretend. We could keep my pink room like it is, with piled up dolls n' shit you bought. For when case workers come by? You know me by now, I'd be cool. I could pretend I slept in there. 'Think I haven't had mommies and uncles and cousins and "best friends" take me in their bed before? Think I'd freak, findin' out you're like them? Haven't you got it by now? Nothing freaks me out. You want stuff, I want stuff. You could still keep getting payments from the State. You gotta like those, every Mom I ever had did.

    (winks)

And like yours just said said, "Show your gratitude, the Universe blesses..."

The Dew Point

Neena Beber

Dramatic
Phyllis, 30s

> *Phyllis is laying into her friend Mimi about her relationship with Jack. Mimi*
> *apparently does understand what a jerk Jack is.*

PHYLLIS: You know what I think is the sickest thing of all? Not him—not
his behavior—but yours. This is a man who decimates women. Who
annihilates them. Who is an absolute liar and who trashes one woman
after another with his lies. He draws them in, seduces, pulls the rug out
from under. He does this on a regular basis and you condone it. you don't
condemn it. Would you be friends with a racist? How about a Nazi? A
charming little Jew-hater from the S.S.? I don't think so. But women, if
the victim is women...

> *(downing the rest of the drink)*

You hide under your convenient little "I won't judge another" mantra
and then you push him onto a friend, you encourage it, even now you
sit there arranging a way for him to continue... you're his goddam pimp.
How about a wonderful, lovely, smart, funny, fabulously engaging man
who just happens to have this one little thing—his predilection for
raping kindergartners? I think he's extreme. I think excusing his behavior
is extreme. Great guy, happens to drive women to the brink of suicide.
I'm sure you'll figure out a rationalization. He fucked you over, what is
it, your goal to see to it that someone else gets fucked over, too? You can
rationalize it all very nicely if you choose. How easy. How simple for
you. It must be lovely to have a brain so well programmed to block out
anything that doesn't fit into your good opinion of yourself.

The Dew Point

Neena Beber

Dramatic
Greta, 30s

Greta is talking to a girlfriend, Mimi, about her complicated relationship with her boyfriend, Jack.

GRETA: I know Jack's a fucker sometimes. But he's afraid. It was getting too real with us, and he got afraid. We store fear in our bodies, we store the fear and the hurt, and there are acupressure points for that.
(Greta goes through a series of dance postures, starting with a relaxed, graceful stretch and becoming increasingly aggressive and agitated.)
I love him with everything I've got, how many people get to love that way? I see the fear and the hurt places and I have a lot of compassion in my heart for him because my background, it was not what you would call in any way "positive." Jack and I share that. We're soul mates, me and Jack. You don't give that up just because a guy puts his dick in the wrong place when he starts to freak.
(Greta ends her routine with a kick and jab in Mimi's direction.)
I'd rather confront him on neutral territory. I know I'm a confrontational person. I'm a dancer. I have to confront stuff all the time. Pain. My own limitations. The music. I have this relationship to music where I kind of, like, confront it.
(Greta offers up another jabbing dance gesture.)
I don't mind a good struggle. Maybe that's why I really don't mind Jack. Why I really believe it will work out, until it isn't meant to work out anymore, but I just don't believe Jack and I are at the end of what we have to work out together and learn from each other yet. See, my problem is I can't lie. Not even to myself. Sometimes I think I'm the only person I know who can't and that makes it pretty much of a bitch sometimes.

The Dew Point

Neena Beber

Dramatic
Mimi, 30s

> *Mimi made the mistake of believing that her boyfriend, Jack, was actually serious about her. She has finally seen the truth about what a jerk he is, and here she lays into him.*

MIMI: You liar. You fucking liar. Why did you do this? Is it a fucking game to you? You beg me to move in with you, beg me to live here when I didn't even want to, I wanted to wait but you push and you push and you wear me down so that what, so you can fuck every fat bitch whore like Lisa who comes your way right under my nose? Who else, you fuck? Annie? Stephanie? Nicole? You did, didn't you, that night you went to dinner with Nicole, a five hour dinner in a restaurant, it's fucking impossible to spend five hours at a Chinese restaurant. You're a walking fucking disease, you've put me at risk, at risk of dying, you fucking sick sick fuck.

(he starts to go)

Where are you going? You're not going to leave me. This is what you've done to me. This is what you've turned me into. I'm reduced. Fucking reduced. I trusted you. I trusted people. I believed in people. This is what you've destroyed. Now I go digging around in your things like an animal, like a fucking sad pathetic rodent going through your garbage, your fucking garbage you're a soul killer, that's what you are a soul killer. Go, you fuck. Just go. Go destroy somebody else you fucking monster.

The Divine Sister

Charles Busch

Comic
Mother Superior, 40's

Mother Superior is a lovely, dignified woman, haunted by her past. She's confronting Mrs. Levinson, a wealthy dowager, who she is convinced is her long lost mother.

MOTHER SUPERIOR: Mrs. Levinson, alas, there is much to be said. It seems that an old charwoman at our school was many years ago in your employ as a maid. At that time, she came across papers detailing an infant's admission to a San Francisco orphanage. The baby's date of birth was August 23, 1926. That is the day I was born and I was raised in that very same institution. The great coincidence is that our paths should cross again. I am fully convinced that you are my mother and that you abandoned me when I became an inconvenience. Erasing me from your life this time will not be as simple. That selfish act condemned me to a loveless childhood in a brutal, sadistic institution. Oh, I could level you with guilt if I told you all that I suffered at the hands of Mr. and Mrs. Carothers, the couple who ran the orphanage, but I won't. I can't do that. Such revenge is contrary to my faith. Oh, I could give you eternal nightmares if I revealed how the drunken Mr. Carothers would dress up as a red devil with horns and a pitchfork and use me as his child whore in the most perverse of sexual bacchanalia. But I won't. That would be too easy. Oh, I could tell you things about the Carothers' degenerate erotic calisthenics involving a bicycle pump, rubber cement and Purina's Cream of Wheat. But I won't. By any account, I should have gone mad. Perhaps I was mad. But through it all, I clung to the fantasy that my mother lived, that she was somewhere in the world, caring and affectionate, regretting her fatal decision and wanting me returned to her loving arms. You can never know what it's like to forever think of yourself as an unwanted orphan. There is always the sense of something missing. An essential puzzle piece lost. You can try to replace it with other things, other beliefs, but nothing can ever fit. You are hard. Why did I come here? I don't know. I suppose I longed to hear some words of regret. Or experience a brief moment of maternal tenderness. But I see that you are incapable of those human feelings.

Dramatis Personae

Gonzalo Rodriguez Risco

Dramatic
Marla, late 20s

Marla is a writer. She's been part of a writers group that meets regularly to discuss their progress and offer each other support, but the situation changes when, across the street from the place where they meet, a terrorist group bombs the Prime Minister's house and takes hostages, including Marla's estranged ex-husband, Julian. At this point in the play they've been trapped in this apartment in the middle of a shoot out for many hours, but they've spent the night talking about writing and creativity, consciously ignoring the terrible situation that surrounds them. Marla, spent by the night's events, suddenly decides to face the truth behind her writing and her marriage, and confronts her fellow writers.

MARLA: I like that word. Trigger. It's a bit ironic to mention it in the middle of a shoot-out, but maybe that's the point... Aim the gun, pull the trigger, and then deal with the consequences. Forget Anton and his stupid wife. Let's talk about Julian. It's been twenty-five days since he was taken hostage, and I've managed to mention him, maybe, three times. Not bad for a disgruntled ex wife. This may be the story behind every single divorce: Married too young. Constant disagreements and fights... I don't know if there was any cheating. Honestly, I don't care... I was hurt by a bad relationship, I met Julian, the "safe guy", and I married him... Not my brightest moment. I woke up one night... We'd had a fight earlier and had just gone to bed without speaking. We were back to back. I wasn't mad anymore, so I was turning to face him when I heard a sigh. Very low. He was weeping. His body was trembling slightly, and I could hear him breathing in little gasps, but he was also trying to be as quiet as possible. He didn't want to wake me... My first thoughts were: I should pretend to sleep. I have to work tomorrow. I don't want to deal with him... So I didn't. I kept still. And I didn't cry. The next day, when he came back from work, I was gone. He didn't deserve it. He was too nice for me, I mean, he married a writer... He should've known how selfish we are. How impossibly self-centered. Just look at us, we're here talking about characters and plots and feelings while seven floors away real people are going through something we could never imagine. Or recreate. And he's one of them. He's a hostage... So I'm worried about him. And the only way I can picture him right now is sitting in a corner in that house, crying in silence, so that his new captors won't notice. So he's not Anton and I'm not the wife. But it might be the other way around... I don't like that.

Dusk Rings a Bell

Stephen Belber

Dramatic
Molly, 39

Molly is describing her night with Ray, a man she only recently met again after having spent an afternoon together as teenagers 24 years earlier.

MOLLY: I go home with him that night; and we make the kind of love that I really like to make. His little "condominium" is way overheated so we're both really sweaty, hugely sweaty, and not just our foreheads; everywhere; I'm sweaty under my arms, between my tits, up inside my thighs; my -- my coccyx is sweaty. It's phenomenal. The whole thing satiates my need for freakishness, because Ray is, Ray obviously has issues, like, I dunno, untapped reserves of violence that he maybe feels bad about never having tapped into, which makes for a sort of lingering, shimmering sense of aggressiveness that is invigorating, slightly scary, but completely unaimed, I think, at me. He's never threatening, he's just wound like an exceedingly compressed coil, for a theoretically calm and repentant guy. It's like---I don't wanna be too, but---it's like he's fucking me with this innate sort of need to make a point that his life has not been a complete and utter waste. He's so needy and inside me, he's so hyper-intensely inside me that it's, I start to shake thinking about it. It's like he's so desirous of bodily contact that I And I come like...like I'm – I dunno – like a Depression era dam that finally gives way to time---and completely just blows its gourd and flows like the first time ever. *(Pause.)* Which is what also makes me cry. And I'm not a crier, I'm really not. But as I'm finishing my little... explosion, this guy is touching my face like … like we're literally the last two people on earth and we've just discovered each other after decades of wandering the barren earth alone, and he's spotted me across the nuclear-scorched, devastated plain of the earth. And he touches my cheek like he's lost all language and yet he just wants to say hello, like a fucking deaf, mute, PTSD'd war refugee on psychotropic drugs. *(pause; quieter:)* All he wants to say is hello.

Easter Monday

Hal Corley

Seriocomic
Adela, mid-30s

A shy, unprepossessing Washington, DC secretary, Adela has come to New York City for the first time to see the Easter flower show — and meet the grown son she gave up for adoption twenty years ago who recently found her on-line. Overwhelmed by stories of the cozy holiday rituals in her son's childhood, she examines a filigreed Christmas ornament with a sense of wonder, and recalls her own austere religious upbringing in Virginia.

ADELA: I never had one a' these. 'Cause Quakers think decorations turn the birth of the Lord into a false idol. We called ourselves "The Friends" back when I was one. We never had pretty stuff like this 'round, but this big family 'cross the street did. They made paper chains at Christmas and strung popcorn and cranberries to put on a pine tree the daddy dug up hisself from some farm out near Middleburg. They had this record of Chipmunks singin' about Christmastime not bein' late. When somebody told me it was just a regular buncha grown-ups singers, played at a fast speed to make the voice sound all squeaky thataways, I didn't believe 'em. I wanted to think there actually were these chipmunks who had 'emselves a chipmunk Christmas. I was little, I didn't know Chipmunks couldn't talk, let alone sing about Christmas or any other thing. I think I cried, finding out. The family invited me to go to their church one Christmas eve, and I was gonna. I'd one time snuck into a church, and hid in back, and seen all these satin shelves of candles. The Friends meetin's just take place in a basement, so the candles were what I wanted to see again. But Quakers are afraid of Catholics, and when Mama found out, she locked me in my room. I got so mad, I banged on the door, and when she ignored me, just using my fists, I started usin' my head, to make me a bigger sound, pounding and pounding. My forehead got bruised and on Christmas morning, when we went to the Friends meeting, I looked like I'd been beat to a pulp, and my ears started ringing. Truth is, I'd done it to myself. I still got a dent up here, from that, and every now n' then my ears still ring. They rang the other night, after I left here.
(Beat.)
The daddy in the family sometimes gave me "surprises," too. Even though

Mama wouldn't let me keep 'em, that was okay. Only time I really liked toys was in stores. In boxes. With clear cellophane over the faces of the dolls or what-have-you. Toys kept way up, on a high shelf, so the cellophane didn't even have fingerprints on it.

(*Beat.*)

That's why I gave away that doll I won. Sometimes I wish I'd known a child to give it to, and that I coulda watched her play with it. But children are s' loud and move too fast and make me nervous.

Flower Duet

Maura Campbell

Dramatic
Stephanie, 30

Stephanie dresses as a man to surprise her husband, with whom she has a vague, open door relationship. He has rejected her and confronted her about his suspicion that she has been unfaithful with one of their friends.

STEPHANIE: I'm tired of trying to figure out how to keep up with you I just want someone to lust after me you know my smell the way I look when I don't care it's humiliating okay okay I thought about it for one fleeting shining moment I thought it would be fun sometimes a girl needs a little fun but I wasn't I'm not it was stupid to even consider when on the other hand I can sit around and watch you smoke pot all week and play with your pictures You don't care whether I sleep with Sandy you don't really care what I do you just don't want to miss out on the fun well guess what it was fun I had two orgasms real ones the kind that can happen between a man and a woman alone together no props no costumes my skin for some men that's enough

Ghosts in the Cottonwoods

Adam Rapp

Seriocomic
Shirley, late teens-early 20s

Shirley has been dating a rather dim young man named Pointer Scully, who lives with his mother in a cabin in the woods. She has come over to tell Pointer that she is pregnant.

SHIRLEY: Feel how warm my belly is, Pointer? It's like somethin's cookin in there, ain't it? *(To Bean)* Missus Scully, Pointer and I are lovers of the most devastatin degree. And I intend on marryin him and raisin our baby together. It all starts with a little bee buzzin around a flower, Missus Scully. Then the summer breeze just makes things ripe and somethin sweet gets in the air, and fish start swimmin backwards and dogs start howlin, and the fire chief starts invitin folks over to the firehouse, and love starts flowin like that slow July breeze. I knew the minute I laid eyes on Pointer that we would forge a union of bewildering desire and violet passion. He was settin up in a tree on Denorfia Memorial Boulevard and I saw that head glowing in the twilight and those long skinny legs danglin over the branches. You coulda hit me with a skillet and I wouldn'ta known the difference. My momma says that kinda feelin don't come by but once. We been meetin each other nearly every day down by the fishpond, haven't we, Pointer? He's told me stuff he ain't never told no one. Thoughts that he has. His philosophy on Hip-hop Music. How bein sexy ain't nothin more than a walk and a talk and a way of settin in a chair. He's told me true stories, too. Like about what his daddy did to him and how he died and how you always go around tellin folks he fell into a hole. And how you're afraid to go outside. I know about all that, Missus Scully. It don't matter to me. I love Pointer anyways. We pledge our love with johnson grass. And sometimes we go skinny dippin. And the troutfish swim under our private parts. And sometimes we'll climb up in a tree and eat leaves. One day we ate thirty-four leaves. We fed em to each other, back and forth. Just like Adam and Eve musta done. That's when we did it. Right on the branch of that tree. That's when we made our baby, ain't it Pointer? And every day I can feel it growin in me. At first I pitchered it like a baby chick. All blond and soft. Then I started seein it like a little fluffy kitten. I would sing to it and meow.

And sometimes I would pretend like it was meowin back at me. Then it turned into a puppy with floppy ears. And now it's a baby horse. A tiny one. Smaller than a fist. And soon it'll be a little Pointer in my stomach. With a beautiful vanilla-butterscotch bald head and big baggy basketball shorts. And I'll play classic hip-hop ceedees every night before I go to bed. Jungle Brothers. Black Sheep. De la Soul. Poor Righteous Teachers. And I'll feel my baby's smile ticklin the inside of my belly. A little Pointer. Even if it's a girl I know it'll come out to be just like Pointer. I'll just name her Pointy.

(Shirley suddenly starts to sing in a high, melodious voice.)
For every flower
There's a summer song and it floats up
to the trees
For every desert There's a water pond
where a drink
is drunk for free
For every rowboat There's a fisherman who cries into the sea
And all my nights
I dream of daffodils cause I know
you're here with me.

Girls in Trouble

Jonathan Reynolds

Dramatic
Sunny, 27, can be either white or African-American.

Sunny is from a poverty-stricken neighborhood. here, she addresses a cafe crowd over a microphone in what resembles a poetry slam.

(Sunny enters, plugged into a Walkman. She can be either white or African-American and she is 27. It is 1983.)

SUNNY: Nooooo, you poppin' shit pompous, booty-ass braggin', tongue-clickin', dick-down, chunky thigh big-ass, bounce like my ace toon coon! You can't treat me like this, you shit!

That first night, you club me, you bling me, you come on to me all

Rolly on my wrist

Champagne pourin' from your fist

Golden rubies on my mind

cause you talkin' so fine—

All sharp and spif, you ain't no bamma from Alabama, I know what I'm seein'—

Pieced up,

Creased up,

Stayin' dressed

to impress

No cable round your neck, 45 malt breeze not good enough for you, you buy me Chandon, then Dom Perignon, woo, too good for me, Danny. I just a po' little ghetto girl nigger born and bred, ain't played 'afore in your ballpark. But you, eyes all soulful, you say, "Sunny, you special," you say, well lots say that, "you special," and I know they after these bubbles, but you, Danny, you say, "Sunny, you special to me. To me!"

And I swole up and look in your soft eyes. You all milk dipped in butter, so smooth, and drip that sugar on me, and my magenta soul just melt, and a course I had you back in the bricks, be braining you all night, don't you never sleep? Juiced till I had no fluid left in my entire body! One month, then three, most nights, and I'm just deeper and deeper into you. But then it commences to begin. I can tell you not quite there with me so much. You fade me, Danny. Two weeks I can't get a nod--you diss me, Danny, treat me like dogfood. Then I know: I embarrassin' you. "Sunny, you don't have to talk street," you say, all Prince Charles or somesuch, but you know I growed up in the hood, same as you, and you think I don't wanna get out? I could shake hands with Nancy Reagan and those two-inch hips, I look good in red, I can get all high society with the Empress of Japan and whatnot. But how'm'I s'posed to do that?

You take me there? But no, you goin' all Upnose on me and wanna leave me behind.

Then what DOOO you know? Miss a month...miss another month... then what's His name, yo' Christian friend intervene.

Then he hit the seed
To some a good deed
And from out the sky
Hear a little cry—
--Waa, Waa—
Life on the march!

And things take a little turn...and who's got the power now, dog? I do-- women do. If I decide and me and me alone to have Danny Junior--and ho, it's all up to me--I could dee-stroy your life. For twenty-one years! You have to support this kid for twenty-one years if I tells you to, that's the law! Everything! Ha ha ha--you gonna pay for not lovin' me. Rich! Rich!

And so uh course you bust on the scene last night, and out comes Barry White again, all dripping sugar. Fool, you think I don't see through that? Only...you tell me...you want the kid! "It would give my life meaning, Sunny." Excuse me? How you'd love a little boy and then a little girl and then another little girl and a coupla more boys and maybe another girl to even it out. And how you'd take care of me as their mother forever, I would never have nothing to worry about. I start to melt again. but then I check and I axe myself, "he jivin' me to get me to get rid of it?" But no, you mean it! "I want to teach them music," you say, "perch 'em on my shoulder." Only you forget one thing. You forget to say you love <u>me</u> or could love <u>me</u>. You supposed to love me first, then them. You gonna use me like a cow to get what you want, no thought of me. You maybe don't even like me at all!

So you know what? I'm gonna take this thing you say you love most and show you where the power at now. There is no fucking way little Danny Junior's coming into this world to delight you, roll its eyes at you, give your life a purpose where there was none except Walkmans and VCRs. You'll never get this--this is mine to do with what I want, and I sure as hell don't want it. I've got three goddam words for what you did to me,

Danny. A-BOR-SHUN. Shit, my momma used to do abortions for a living right here in Cleveland when it was illegal, nothin' to it, 'cept for that once. How could you not love me? How could you not? I'd'a done anything for you!

So go on, tell me once more how much it would mean to you to have a little boy, walk him to school every day, teach him basketballin' and the trom-fucking-bone, read him stories at night. Here's the haps, Danny: No! And you think I won't do it? I snaps cats' necks!

(NB* This role was intended to be played by either a white or an African-American actress, and if played by a white actress, the word "nigger" should be changed to "wigger." Nothing else.)

Goodbye New York Goodbye Heart

Lally Katz

Dramatic
Miss Jacklyn, 30s

Miss Jacklyn is in her mid thirties. She dresses as though she were younger, but it only makes her look older. In this monologue she is at a party hosted by the Fox in the Box Cafe, and she is speaking to members of the Avalanche Dwellers Anonymous Society, of which she is president. The Avalanche Dwellers are a group of people who have left their own lives, in order to live in internet cities with their beloved family members, friends and lovers who are suicides. Miss Jacklyn often makes speeches to the other Avalanche Dwellers here in MySpace New York, expressing the feeling of devotion and love both she and they feel for the suicides.

MISS JACKLYN: I'm ravaged. I've hoped for so many. I've found so few who have stayed. By my side. In a rose bed of hidden thorns. And I asked all those that I loved to lie down there. With their neckaches, I said, 'I will massage you.' But with hands like these? Gardner's groper's hands with pointed nails. How can I touch a thing so pure and good? Do you know who I mean? How can I touch a face that isn't copying an angel? It just is. Those sweet wings behind his shoulder blades. That all those whores could touch with their arms reached up behind his back. I know things of him- histories- which he would kill anyone for having said out loud, and none of it is my business, and all of his past moments do not belong to me and will never be in my hands- but that I love him- that even now my insidious heart longs to turn him to my army. Is there a thought crueller than that one? To make him love me? To make an angel cursed to love me. I hate myself even to wish it. Even to walk by his lawn and drizzle pigeon food is a sin. I drink my homemade café latte. I change my own light bulbs. But for what? I have seen nothing in this world but the glow of his cheek when he smiles. Oh, this lonely window. From my hallway, to the world.

Grace

Craig Wright

Dramatic
Sara, 30's

> *Sara, a married woman with a strong belief in her Christian faith, has been*
> *making regular visits to her next door neighbor Sam, a non-believer whose*
> *girlfriend died in a terrible car accident that left his face badly scarred. As*
> *Sara and Sam fight against their desire for each other, she relates to him the*
> *story of the first time she had a personal, religious experience as a 13 year old*
> *at Bible Camp.*

SARA: There was a guest speaker at camp all week. His name was Ed Stube.
And I went the first night to the big welcome, you know, prayer service,
where it was like, "We're all here to have fun and the pancakes'll be good
and Jesus, y'know…wow!" You know, my family, we went to church,
but it never really meant anything that big to me. It was a part of my
life, I had friends there, but that was it. But then this guy Ed Stube got
up and started showing his slide show about how he was a missionary in
Micronesia. And he had slides of the countryside and the terraced hills
and all that stuff. His church. His congregation. And then up came this
slide of, like, a ten-year-old girl. *(after a beat)* And I swear, I could feel the
elevator drop inside me, just looking in her eyes. Boom. Straight to the
bottom. I had no idea why. But then he said, "This is a girl I raised from
the dead." The picture was… I mean, I really had to admit, there was
something about it. There was something very weird. There was a fire in
the background about ten yards away with people all around it. And this
girl was in the foreground, staring into the camera. Just a girl. But she
had this look in her eyes of the most compassionate …interest. I'd never
seen anything like it. I'm not really explaining this well, probably. All I
want to say is: that night, after the preaching, Ed Stube asked if anyone
wanted to come down for the altar call, and, you know, "accept Jesus into
their hearts," which is something I never would have done, I didn't even
know what it meant…but I did it. I went down and prayed the prayer
[and someone was listening]. No, not someone. It wasn't a someone.
It was more like Everything Else was listening. But it was more than
Everything Else. Like the Everything Else was a Someone. Somehow.
(after a beat) And ever since that night, Sam, I can't help it, there is this

big music I hear in things, like everything in the world is all one big music and I'm part of it. And I know no one can convince anyone of anything with words, that's fine, they shouldn't be able to. I don't want to change anybody. I just want to tell you, this is how I see things. If you're ever going to tell yourself you knew me, you need to know that. That's how I see things. And I don't know what you've been, or been like, I just know you now. And I know you don't believe in anything like what I'm talking about. And that's okay. But I want you to know that I feel like getting to know you -- having the chance -- has been a way God has filled my life a little, when I really needed it -- and shown me something new and scary and possible, and I'm glad it's happened. I'm glad we've met, I'm glad I've come over here. *(after a beat)* And I just want you to be happy because I think you're great. That's all. That's all.

Grand Cayman

Don Nigro

Seriocomic
Mary, 20s

> *Mary, an attractive young woman in her twenties, wearing a bikini, has sat down on a deck chair on the beach, on the island of Grand Cayman, in the Caribbean, between two very tough looking guys in suits, Murphy and Antonelli, who May be private detectives or hit men, we're not sure. She says she's just sat there to scare off some men who've been annoying her, but it becomes clear that something more than that is going on. They've been hired to follow an old man named Leo, and she's been Leo's companion. It would appear that she's realized she's being watched, and wants to make them some sort of a deal. She suggests that she has access to an obscene amount of money, and begins to talk about the relationship between money and violence. She seems to be enjoying teasing them, making them uncomfortable, and even perhaps the excitement of being in danger herself.*

MARY: There are plenty of people in this world who kill for money. They track people down and kill them like rabbits. Of course, some people kill for pleasure, but I'm not talking about them. I'm talking about professionals. You guys have been around the block once or twice. You've probably met people like that. It's not surprising that these people exist, considering the evolutionary history of our species. What I find interesting is what the limits are. Where such a person would draw the line. Maybe one sort of assassin would only kill men, but another wouldn't mind killing women. Or another might draw the line at children. And there's probably some who don't mind killing people but would never hurt a dog. And then some people would do anything for money, kill anybody, even a friend, even their own brother. What's really interesting is where exactly a person would say, I'll do this, but not that. I'm not talking about risk factors. That would certainly be a legitimate consideration, but that's just good business. I'm talking about moral reservations, whether it's about killing a woman or a child or how many people at once, or about killing a member of their family. Or would they have reservations about their immediate family, but knocking off a third or fourth cousin or an in-law would be okay? Or would it be okay to kill anybody as long as you've got a uniform on and somebody told you to? Do you see what I'm getting at here? Here's an example. You guys are friends, right? Let's just, for the sake of argument, presume that you're friends. You might get on each other's nerves once in a while, but you guys have been working together a long time, say. Maybe you even grew up together in the old neighborhood—Brooklyn or Jersey or Cleveland or wherever. So you're close. You might not want to admit it, but you take care of each other. You rely on each other in dangerous situations. You've even killed for each other, at one time or another. So my question is, say, if some hypothetical person offered one of you an obscene amount of money, would he be willing to kill the other one?

Gruesome Playground Injuries

Rajiv Joseph

Dramatic
Kayleen, 20s

> *Kayleen has come to the hospital to visit her accident-prone friend Doug, who lies in a hospital bed in a coma, the result of his latest mishap. Kayleen and Doug are soul-mates, but they just don't see it. Here, Kayleen pleads with the inert Doug not to die. She has always helped him recover from his various injuries. Will she be able to save him this time?*

KAYLEEN: You can't marry that girl, Doug. You can't. Because what about me? What about me, huh?

When my Dad died, when you... when you came to the funeral home that night...

That stuff you said to me...

You're always doing that, you know? The top ten best things anyone's ever done for me have all been done by you. That's pretty good, right?

And I know. I know I know I know...

I'm so stupid. I'm always...

I'm just fucked up, you know that.

And so I need you to stick it out, Dougie.

I'm gonna need you to come looking for me again.

I'm sorry. But you have to wake up now. You have to wake up for me. Because I'm not great, you know?

I'm not great.

And I really need you right now. I really need you to come over and show me some stupid shit again, tell me some stupid joke like you always do.

I'm sorry I've been gone. I'm back now. You know? I'm back now. So wake up.

Wake up now, buddy.

Just, you know... rise and shine. It's Tuesday.

That was always your favorite day.

The Housewives of Mannheim

Alan Brody

Dramatic
Billie, 29

Billie is a 29 year old housewife in a Brooklyn apartment house in 1944, during World War II. The night before, she made love to her straight friend, May, for the first time. May feels betrayed and Billie tries to make her understand how she felt.

BILLIE: May? Did you feel something for me? I've always imagined what it must feel like to be you. Did you EVER imagine what it's like to be me? Even a little?
   (May does not repond)
You live your life having to be so careful- - - I'm trying to tell you something. About me. You live your life having to be so careful. You have to keep it all to yourself, and you're growing up and there's no one in the movies who feels like you do, and no one in the magazines or on the radio or in the lending library. The only time you hear about anyone is in the Daily Mirror and they report on somebody who murdered her husband. They don't even come out and say it. They just hint something was wrong, and you're maybe only thirteen, but you know what they mean, that she was like you and she was bad. And you start to hate yourself for not being able to be like other people and you start hating other people because you're afraid they might find out. So you make them laugh instead. You're not even in high school yet, but you've figured out that's how to survive. And then one day, you meet another woman, and you know she knows. And at first you're afraid, but you want a friend so much you say yes when she asks if you want to go to a movie. And little by little you find out there are others. You're not so alone after all, and when you're with them, even though it has to be in secret, you don't have to be so careful. And you figure you're going to be all right, you can work it out, you can even have the kid you always wanted. But then, from out of nowhere, comes another woman, not like you, and you fall in love. You have to be careful again. You have to be satisfied just to be her friend and you tell yourself that's enough. You love her that much that you don't want to take the chance, don't want to spoil anything. At first when I saw you with Sophie I was jealous. But then I thought if

she finds out she can love another woman, then maybe there's a chance for me. So I took another chance. And I thought, I don't care if this is a mistake. *(Pause)* Maybe it was a mistake. Just don't hate me the way I used to hate myself.

In the Wake

Lisa Kron

Dramatic
Judy, 40's-50's

Judy is a hard-bitten international aid worker who has recently returned to the States and who is staying with her friend Ellen, a political activist who is more talk than action. Judy has not only talked the talk but she's also walked the walk, and here she tells Ellen what it has cost her.

JUDY: Look, Ellen, the idea that the system leads to a place for everyone is a myth. There has never been a place for everyone. It's only the people who benefit from that who think there is. But the people at the top are the same people who've always been at the top. And the people who are at the bottom are the same people who've always been at the bottom. I see a system that adjusts to maintain that order. Occasionally a door cracks open for a decade or so and then it gets slammed shut. Reconstruction lasted twenty years and was crushed by Jim Crow. Johnson's War on Poverty was actually working. You know that, right? Nixon put Rumsfeld and Cheney in charge of it and told them to strangle it. It's all documented. It's no secret. Poor people aren't even part of the political discussion any more. Have you noticed that? What I see in the wake of Civil Rights is the population of Black men exploding in prison. I see less access to health care, to public schools, to all sorts of public amenities. All the things you rail about. It's not coincidental that those things are being privatized, being put into the hands of fewer people with more money, and taken out of the public sector. Poor people and Black people are suffering and that's not an anomaly. That's written into the system. I'm an exception that proves the rule. I had a tremendous amount of luck. People who crossed my path, teachers and so forth who pulled me onto a different track. That's luck. Plus I was smart. If you're poor and you're smart you might get out. Rich people don't have to be smart. Middle class people don't either. I'm saying that for some people there is no more potential here. You're a middle class person and you are served well by the system so you have to believe that change is possible. It's what American liberals do. Because what could you do otherwise? You'd have to give up your middle class life or your ideals. Look at my sister staying with a man who beats her. Look at my mother, sabotaging herself and her kid at every turn. You know that stereotype of welfare dependency the right wing loves talk about? That's my family. Do I look at them and think they're fuck-ups? Yes. Do I blame them for the fact that Tessa couldn't keep it together long enough to just get a lousy high school diploma? Yes. That girl broke my fucking heart. I'm ashamed of my family. It's unbearable to me. I can hardly even get the words out of my mouth because I'm ashamed of being ashamed. The political line on them is they just aren't trying hard enough. They don't believe in themselves. And it's true. And why? Because they don't have that sense of aspiration you're talking about. Because they live in an America where if you can't get the paperwork you're told you need for the forms someone tells you have to fill out you are shit out of luck. They live in an America that is configured to keep them right where they are. And if you grow up in that place you understand that -- and if you don't, you don't. You talk about what people take for granted -- you take for granted your own worth - you take for granted that you are worthy of love. Who but someone who completely believes in that could live the way you've lived? Who else could make the choices you've made? You can criticize marriage and have "expansive" thoughts about relationships, not because you think the system of marriage is wrong but because you don't need it -- you don't need to be reassured you won't be left! Most people, they don't know that. They don't believe that. Look at how shocked you are. How can that be the case? How did you get this far in life without having your heart broken?

The Language Archive

Julia Cho

Seriocomic
Mary, 30s

Mary owns and operates a bakery. Here, she is talking to a woman who has come in to check out her shop, who has asked her how she became a baker

MARY: Well, quite recently, I left my husband.
(A shadow crosses her face, briefly.)
That was a hard time. It sounds strange to say it, but the truth was, I was sad. I'd simply become too sad to stay. So I left. I left without much. Just a suitcase. And I really didn't have a plan. And then, I was at the train station, wondering where I should go. And there was an old man there. He asked me for the time and we started talking. He told me he was a baker but that he was leaving his bakery. Why, I asked him. He told me he was tired of baking bread. He had never wanted to be a baker. But his father had been a baker and his father's father had been a baker and so on and so forth—his last name was actually "Baker" if you can believe it. Anyway, this man told me he'd decided enough was enough. He locked up his bakery, put up a sign that said, "Closed until further notice," and he was off. Then I noticed he was carrying a very odd box and I've always been the curious type so I asked him what was in it. And he sighed a great sigh and said it was the one thing he could not leave behind. It was his inheritance, the most precious thing he owns. It was his starter. All bread, you see, comes from a starter. The most common is the yeast you buy in little packets at the supermarket. But it's alive, you know; it's a living organism. And truly great bread comes from truly great starters. The older a starter, the richer, more complex it is. Back in my baking days I'd heard tales of starters handed down from generation to generation—ancient starters that had been kept alive for years, for decades! But keeping a starter alive takes time. You have to feed it, watch it, make sure it doesn't die. And this poor man had been tethered to his starter. His father had passed it on to him, made him the keeper of the starter. How could he abandon it? And as I heard this story, I got a strange little tingling feeling in my chest. I heard myself say: "Give me your starter! Let me take care of it!" And as soon as I heard myself say it, I understood that it was nothing less than my heart's truest desire. I

wanted this starter. I wanted to bake bread! And I have no idea why, but the man must have seen something in me he trusted. Because he gave me his starter; he gave me the keys to this bakery. And now he is off, traveling the world, just like he always wanted. And that is how I wound up here, baking bread. Isn't that a marvelous story?

Lascivious Something

Sheila Callaghan

Dramatic
Daphne, 23

Daphne is a beautiful Greek woman who lives on a small secluded island in the Ionian Sea with her much older ex-pat American husband, August. Out of nowhere, an old love of August's shows up on their island with an unnamed agenda. Here, Daphne describes to this woman her understanding of a moment from her husband's past.

DAPHNE: You and he were living out of your small car at the San Francisco Bay. You had no more food. You had not washed yourselves in two weeks besides your feet in the water. You had sex four times a day and were on pot much of the time. You were lying with your stringy head in his lap with your eyes closed.. You were talking about molecules moving in your fingers and your feet. You were talking about how your skin was not solid, how the vinyl seat was not solid. You said everything was vibrating in nature at all times, and you said it scared you so much, and you said the only time you felt still was when his voice was in your ears, low and serious. And then you felt a wet drop on your closed lids, and you opened them and he was crying into your eyes. And he said you are so beautiful Liza, you are so beautiful you could crack the sky open. And you said August you are like the universe, you are so big you fill me you fill my ears and you fill me. He brought his head down to yours and unrolled his tongue into your mouth. And his fingers wound around your hair. And you grabbed his hip with your hand and you said the word NEED, and you wrapped your thick leg around his skinny leg and said the word NEED, and then you sank your teeth into his hip and bit so hard you came back with part of him in your mouth. And then you made love. And you fell asleep. And when you woke up you had a red smear on your face where you fell asleep in his blood. But he was gone. That was the last time you saw him.

Leaves

Lucy Caldwell

Dramatic
Phyllis, 40s

Phyllis is speaking to her eldest daughter Lori, 19, who has recently returned home from university following a failed suicide attempt.

PHYLLIS: How did we fail you? We fed, and clothed, and loved you - Christ, we loved you - love you - love all of you - we read (Past tense.) stories to you at night - took you to the play- ground and pushed you on the swings - taught you to swim and to ride a bike - helped you with your homework, drove you to music lessons, to ice skating lessons, to your friends' houses - and these sound like little things but they aren't - we hoovered the monsters up from under the bed when you wouldn't believe that they were gone - do you remember that - laughed when you laughed, cried when you cried - were happy so long as you were happy - were happy whenever you were happy. You were every- thing to us. We did everything it was in our power to do for you. We gave you everything it was in our power to give to you. And I know that there have been times when - I mean not for one second am I saying that things have been in any way perfect, because of course there have been tears, and arguments, and - But - Lori - can you tell me - please can you tell me -
(Silence. Lori does not say anything. Phyllis turns and walks away.
Suddenly:)
Well if you're not going to talk to me then let me tell you something, Lori. When you were born -
(She chuckles despite herself)
- there was a woman in the bed across from me who'd just had twins. I can't for the life of me remember her name, now. She was only a year or so older thn I was, but they were her fourth and fifth, she had three others already, all under five I think - can you imagine! I didn't for the life of me know how I was going to manage with just the one. With you. I was terrified. I was too scared to pick you up in case I dropped you. And one night I told this to your woman. And the following day she hatched a grand plan - and I don't know how on earth she managed to persuade me to go along with it - but she did - she had lipstick and heated rollers in her overnight bag, and we dolled ourselves up, did our hair and what

have you - and then when the nurses took the babies away to bathe them, didn't the two of us sneak out of the hospital and into the pub across the way. We had a Bloody Mary each, and your woman turns to me and says, You're going to be alright, so you are, your baby's not going to break. "Your baby's not going to break." Now why I'm telling you this, Lori, why I'm telling this to you - When we got back to the ward visiting hour had begun, and your father was already there, and oh he was furious with me for leaving you, absolutely furious. Anything could have happened, he said, anything - and I started crying, and - and I'm standing there, holding you, like this, just - looking at you, your fingers, and your toes, your eyelashes - everything about you, so - perfect, and I don't know what I've done to deserve you, and I don't know how I can ever, ever be - worthy of you. And all of a sudden I know that I would do anything for you. Anything. I will die for you, I will- And that's something that never changes, something that never goes away, ever - Because there's nothing that can break that bond, nothing, because - because I carried you inside of me, Lori, because - you were and are a part of me.

Let's not Talk about Men

Carla Cantrelle

Seriocomic
Gwen, 20s

Gwen is talking to a married friend about how and why she hates men.

GWEN: Today I hate all of them. Especially the ones I don't know. Them most of all. Because soon I'll know them and they'll do something to make me hate them. But since I don't know them, I don't know what that horrible thing will be. I won't be prepared. And because I'm an idiot, I'll think that everything will be different with them. Because they're new. And I don't know them. At least if you know them, you kind of know where the land mines are. You're married. That's a whole different mine field. Dating. Gack. You think you're blithely strolling through the park but its really the de-militarized zone and poorly defined at that. Then POW! one misplaced reference to some movie that reminds him of his last girlfriend! No warning. Kaplooey! Or one too many "Does this make me look fat" Wham! I just hate them. In fact, I don't even want to think about them. Just once, I'd like to get through a day without even mentioning them. Let's make a pact. For this brunch, let's not talk about men!

Liner Notes

John Patrick Bray

Seriocomic
Alice, 20

Alice is the daughter of a deceased rock-and-roll singer. She is speaking to George, late 40's/early 50's. He was the guitarist for her father's first band, Ghost Light Operator, but was noticeably absent from his funeral. She has just shown up unexpectedly, having driven straight from Montreal to Spartanburg, South CAROLina, to confront George whom she has not seen since she was a very little girl.

ALICE: Hi! *(Beat.)* . I didn't bring coffee. I meant to! It's this place I work at - Cafe Art Java, near the Metro Station. I'm standing there yesterday morning, about to make coffee, and not just coffee for me, but for everybody, I mean my entire part of town shows up at 5:15, even though we don't open until 5:30, but it's this LUNATIC Annie that works there, she opens the door wide open at 3 AM, singing her heart out to Bonnie Tyler or worse, Leonard Cohen, letting all the lunatics just hang out, eating cookies free of charge, and so when people show up at 5:15, they expect their coffee to be ready, and she knows all their orders; BUT, if SHE'S not working, and I'M working, I don't open the store until 5:30, which is when we open; so, I've got a line by 5:25, people banging, literally, BANGING on the glass, pointing to their watches, AND WHAT THE FUCK KIND OF JOBS DO THEY WORK THAT THEY NEED COFFEE BY 5:30? And so, I'm standing, the coffee maker's going, no Bonnie Tyler today, my heart is fucking POUNDING IN MY CHEST, and I can't even look at the book -- and I'm like, FUCK IT! NOBODY GETS COFFEE TODAY! NONE OF YOU GET COFFEE! MONTREAL CAN HAVE A FUCKING LACK-OFCAFFEINE-INDUCING-MIGRAINE FOR ALL I FUCKING CARE! FUCK YOU AND YOUR COFFEE NEEDS YOU FUCKING ADDICTS OF FUCKING - GRRRRRRRRRRRRR! And I get in my car, they're all looking at me with destroyed coffee-less faces, I might as well have killed a cute puppy and dropped it on their heads for the sulking they're doing, as I'm speeding away...and I can't drive home, the carpet needs cleaning, there's dishes, there's MY MOTHer, who, don't worry knows I'm here --and I don't know what to do, so I end up driving here

Local Nobody

Nicole Pandolfo

Comic
Gina, 27

Gina is a cocaine/ pill addict, otherwise pretty, but worn. Really really into Cher. Spends her time at her mother's house or Lou's bar. Here, Gina encounters Sal at a local dive bar. He is clearly uninterested in interacting with her; but unaware of that, she begins to chat him up anyway.

GINA: What are you drinking? Straight, this early in the day? I usually like to start with something light like a chardonnay or a rum and coke, you know? If I start with the straight hard booze I'll be wasted by lunch and then I'll do something stupid like forget to eat the rest of the day. It's actually a pretty good diet. Like if you're trying to lose weight. I love whisky though. A lot. Too much even. I can get kinda out of control when I drink it. Well, when I drink a lot of it. I think it messes with my brain chemistry or something. Just like how people say they get crazy when they drink tequila, I'm like that with whisky. Yeah, I shouldn't drink whisky. *(Pause.)* Can you believe it's this cold out now? Like, shouldn't it be spring? Or at least above freezing. Is it just me or was this winter the worst in history? I mean, pretty much everyone I know is depressed. I'm too anxious to be depressed. Are you depressed? Wouldn't it be cool if you could kill yourself, like for a week? Or maybe even just a weekend. Just to take a break. I'm talking about a vacation. Well since I can't afford a vacation, I think temporary suicide would be an interesting alternative. As long as it was temporary. It's just a fantasy.

Love Letters Made Easy

Jeanne Beckwith

Seriocomic
Diana, about 30.

Diana is speaking to someone who is interviewing her for a documentary or book.

DIANA: He told me that you could not pronounce his name even if your hearing had been enhanced by the sensory preceptors. Our human brain only registers sound input on a quasi-elemental level, and we have no ability to reproduce as sound what is not sound at all. *(Pause.)* Still. I like to call him something. It is so good to whisper something that is sort of like a name. It makes it all seem more *present.* It makes him seem more *present.* I call him Aur-el. I whisper 'Aur-el' when there is no one to hear. Of course, the chip records all. When he downloads my information, he will know that I do this, and it will amuse him. He will not laugh at me though. He would never laugh at me. People from his world do not laugh. Laughter and ridicule are unknown to them. Most of the world laughs at us. *Abductees.* You would too. You would roll your eyes behind my back. Don't think I am unaware of your scorn, but it does not bother me. You have not seen or felt the presence of the visitors. How could you understand? Besides, I think we scare you, and you are very wise to be afraid. When our transformation is complete, you will not ever laugh at us again. I have Aur-el's chip inside my brain. It knows what I know and sends his messages to me. His messages are not quite like words. They have no words in his world. There are no words at all in trans-dimensional space. They have no need for words. There is a kind of singing for them. A communion of colors and soft thin silk against the skin. I have been taken six times. The first time I was seven. They say in the books and on television that there's a bright light, but I remember wind. I remember the wind pushing me back against my pillow. *(Pause.)* Each time they take you, you become a little more capable of making the leap between worlds. The chip implanted in my brain makes it possible for me to know this and understand even though there are no words. I have come to understand how truly useless words are. How incapable they are of ever giving us the truth. This way, I cannot lie to Aur-el, and Aur-el will never lie to me. His thoughts are inside the chip and inside me. There is no way for my mind to escape them. There is a tingling, a buzzing--not a true buzzing. Not like sound. There is no sound. It only starts to vibrate and then to build and build and build. It is sound and not sound, but it is like meaning. It is like being. It is a promise. It is an answer. Aur-el loves me. Or what they do in his world instead of love, better than love. Love is lonely and love destroys. Aur-el protects me from the ones who hurt. He guides and teaches me. When I am wise enough, when I have transformed, I will make the leap into trans-dimensional space. I will see and not see Aur-el. And I will dance.

m

Marble

Marina Carr

Dramatic
Catherine, early 40s.

Catherine is speaking to her husband Ben. It is her final conversation with him. She is leaving him and their children to go off and pursue a dream of Marble.

CATHerINE: Do you believe? Actually believe this sojourn here means something?

Houses, jobs, children, art galleries, theatres, stadiums, wine bars, trees, mountains, birds for god's sake, who can possibly believe in the fact of a bird? They believed it in Babylon, too, and there is no trace of them now. I walk this city and all I see is scaffolding, building, building, building, an avalanche of warrens and ratholes to stuff us in and all I can think of is Troy. And when people ask me for directions in the street, I have to turn away quickly so I don't laugh in their faces. How can they possibly stand there with a map when everything is in such chaotic flux? But they point with their mortal fingers, insisting that such and such a place actually exists to be visited and admired or criticized. Turn left, I say, always left, when what I really want to tell them is, there will be no trace of you or I or that child you hold so lovingly by the hand, a hundred years from now there will be no trace of us, not a whisper, not a puff of ether, we're gone, we were never born. I'm just talking, Ben, about my life. It's not pretty, but it's mine. This is what is happening to me. My reptilian brain is on the ascent, and I'm on a descent, a descent away from some marble room that cannot be reached. Why are we given such images, such sublime yearnings for things that are never there? A dream was given to me, inside me from birth, a dream of marble, a woman in a marble room with her lover. And all the waking world can do is thwart it and deny it, and say, no, it cannot be, childish, impossible, you must walk the grey paths with the rest of us, go down into the wet muck at the close. That's your lot. That's what you have to look forward to. Well, I refuse it, Ben, I refuse it. I refuse this grey nightmare with its ridiculous rules and its lack of primary colours. And I despise you for laying down under it, worse, for embracing it, for being so smug, satisfied with so little.

The Metal Children

Adam Rapp

Dramatic
Vera, teens

> *The local school board is holding a hearing in order to decide whether or not to ban a novel for young adults, which has caused quite a controversy. Here, Vera speaks about what the novel means to her and to many other students, and why it should remain in the curriculum.*

VERA: Thank you, Mr. Hurley. Before I begin, I just have to say that when one is looking to illustrate moral absolutes, it's easy to turn to scripture, a piece of literature that has been translated so many times by so many cultures that some scholars believe it to be the single most mutilated text in the history of the known world. Thank you, Tami, for helping to further facilitate what the Christian Coalition, Toby Keith, Rupert Murdoch, and Fox News have been campaigning so hard for in recent years: to secure our country's swift and relentless return to the Dark Ages. I'll begin now.

(Reading from a piece of paper)

Perhaps art's greatest responsibility in a democracy is to hold a mirror up. Storytelling's function, whether it be spoken by the mouths of actors on a stage or discovered in the pages of books, is not to simply entertain and spread the mind-numbing analgesic that television and video games do so virally, but to show us who we are and what is wrong with the world around us; to help us understand the complexity and confounding realities of what it means to be human. The function of great literary works is not only to amuse but to shake the reader, to present the truth, no matter how grisly or unbearable. Each year, almost one million teenage American women – ten percent of all women aged fifteen-to-nineteen – become pregnant. Fifty-six percent of these pregnancies result in births. Thirty percent in abortions. Fourteen percent in miscarriages. With *The Metal Children*, Mr. Falmouth takes the truth of these numbers and concocts a heart-stopping fable where twenty-three young women at a fictional high school in the American heartland are not only getting pregnant but also inexplicably disappearing. Meredith Miller, the heroine of his novel, martyrs herself and her fetus at the feet of all those statues that we've heard so much about these past weeks. Is this ending painful?

Yes. Is it harrowing? Yes. Did I cry when I read it? Yes. Did it anger me? Yes. It also made me think about my life in a way that I hadn't in a very long time. What if I had sex without a condom and became pregnant? Would I have the child? Would I abort the fetus? Would I give it up for adoption? Would I leave town and never look back? And is the ending explained? Is it carved up and served to its reader like a good Thanksgiving turkey? No. It is difficult and devastating – perhaps savage even – and is left up to the reader to interpret. In my view, Mr. Falmouth's novel is a cutting but keenly observed commentary on the failure of community to find solutions for its younger generation. After the deacon of the local church finds Meredith Miller lying dead in that cornfield, still clutching her father's hunting knife, he doesn't kneel down and pray for her soul or seek the sympathy in his heart; he slaps her. And that's how the book ends. The spiritual leader of Meredith Miller's community slaps her cold, dead face. And that's what's happening here in Midlothia. The school board, in conjunction with the Good Church of Christ and a gaggle of parents shrouded in cloaks of fear, is slapping not only the students from Mr. Kinsella's class who were so moved and inspired by The Metal Children, but every single one of us here tonight. To remove art from a culture is to name that culture dead! I'll say it again! To remove art from a culture is to name that culture dead! In closing, I would like to explain why I am painted gold tonight. Thirty-nine students from Mr. Kinsella's Great Books class are currently standing in the Midlothia Memorial football field. Like me, they are all painted gold. They are all standing very still, I'd even say statue-like, and holding candles as a kind of vigil. After the Assembly, I will join them to become the fortieth student. And I too will hold a candle and stand as still as I can. And we will remain standing across the fifty-yard line for three hours as a protest against the ridiculous and unfortunate confiscation of The Metal Children. And you're all welcome to come by and take in this vision of support for Mr. Falmouth's novel. It's a hundred and ninety-eight pages, and it will rock your world. Meredith Miller lives forever!

Miracle on South Division Street

Tom Dudzick

Comic
Clara Nowak, 65

> *Clara is the caretaker of the family heirloom – a 15-foot shrine to the Blessed*
> *Mother, commemorating the day in 1942 when the Blessed Virgin Mary*
> *materialized in her father's barber shop! In this scene with her children,*
> *Clara is defending the legend to those who would call the miracle a "phoney."*

CLARA: Ruthie, I heard it a thousand times from your Grandma. "Mary wouldn't show her ankles like that!" I know, I know. But your Grandpa wouldn'ta lied, sweetie. He said that's the way she appeared. She musta had her reasons. In the old Bible times, yeah, they wore the long robes and things. But this was the forties. ...Look, honey -- I want you to listen for a second. I want you to think back. Do this for me. Think about what your Grandma was like. Do you remember? Huh? Are you thinkin' about your Grandma? Got a clear picture in your head? Rotten, wasn't she? And who better to say. Now I'm gonna tell you this the one time so you'll understand, and then next Saturday I'll go to confession. 'Cause I ain't had these thoughts or said these words for twenty years. ...Honey, that woman was mean. From as early as I can remember, nasty. Three, four years old I was and she would flick my ears whenever I wasn't lookin'. For no reason! Drove me crazy. Finally hadda wear ear muffs, all year round. They used to call me "Muffy." What it came down to was, she didn't like me. I don't know why. But that's how it was and I lived with it. Told myself, okay, so other people got nice mothers. Lucky them. So what? I got a nice father. And a nice husband and nice kids. That's plenty for me, I'm satisfied. And my kids...they'll never have to go through what I did with that-
>   *(Stops herself.)*
-- with that unhappy woman. So, what I'm saying is, that's exactly the kind of lousy thing your Grandma woulda done. Tell you a story like that at the last minute, to make us think bad about your grandfather. A stinker up to the very end. Gettin' in that last flick. Ruthie, I heard it a thousand times from your Grandma. "Mary wouldn't

Miracle on South Division Street

Tom Dudzick

Comic
Clara Nowak, 65

Clara is the caretaker of the family heirloom – a 15-foot shrine to the Blessed Mother, commemorating the day in 1942 when the Blessed Virgin Mary materialized in her father's barber shop! In this scene, Clara is confronting her children who are suggesting she sell the old inner-city homestead and move to the suburbs.

CLARA: And now I should listen to Lizzie? A girl who skips town at the first sign of trouble? Lizzie's from Lackawanna, what does she know what it was like here once upon a time? Was she here when there was twenty businesses on a block? And families, and kids on bicycles, and dogs? I was here. And your father, he was born here, born right there on Seymour Street, used to tell me all about it. Seymour used to be a canal until they filled it in; didja know that? No! He knew all the history. That canal used to power all the factories around here. They had big water wheels on 'em, catchin' the water to make 'em go. Swan Lounge? Used to be a tannery. Made leather. Right where there's drunks fallin' off their bar stools today, they used to make leather for belts and shoes. Huh? When you hear 'em on Channel 13 talking about our city's history, its industry, it all started right here, kiddo. John Larkin, Elbert Hubbard. How 'bout Frank Lloyd Wright, y'heard o' him? Had a building right over there on Seneca. Those millionaires' mansions on Delaware Avenue, sittin' all empty now, where do you think those guys made their millions? Right here, baby. When they called this city the Second Chicago, it's 'cause o' what happened on these six blocks. So I should listen to Lizzie? What's her brilliant idea, bulldoze the place? I'm tellin' you, you cut out this neighborhood and you'll be cuttin' out the city's heart. ...No sir, movin' away and givin' up is not what you do when your neighborhood's sick. Did I give up on you kids when you were sick? Huh? When you had chicken pox, did I go hoppin' on a bus to Crystal Beach? When you were burnin' with fever, was I off sippin' a sno-cone on the Wild Mouse? ...Face reality, you say. Maybe it's time I reminded you, James Francis Nowak, of the reality of where the Blessed Mother appeared. It was not in Orchard Park or in Lackawanna. She appeared <u>here.</u> Never mind the Larkins and the Hubbards, we're the Nowaks and we live on holy ground. Like it says on my sign out there. "Our Lady's Miracle Soup. Prepared on Holy Ground." If I hung up that sign in Orchard Park I'd be lying! ...Move, he says. You know who else wanted me to move? Leave the statue behind for the garbage men? My own mother! Can you believe it? Said Our Lady never appeared anyway, 'cause no self-respecting saint would appear in a barbershop. Said it's gotta be a grotto or somethin'. Like Fatima. Well, excuse me, I told her, but this is America, we ain't got grottos. We got barbershops. And McDonalds. Any grotto we ever had is a WalMart now. So? So, Mary's a sensible woman, she takes what she can get. She sees a nice empty barbershop – POOF! "Here I am!"

Motherhouse

Victor Lodato

Dramatic
Evelyn, thirties

> *Three years before the play begins, Evelyn's young son was shot, accidentally, while walking with her to church on Mother's Day. Today is the third anniversary of her son's death, and she has just returned from retracing the steps of that tragic walk, a ritual she does every year. here, in reliving the day of the shooting, she is largely speaking to herself, though her mother is present as a witness.*

EVELYN: See now they never found it. That always gets to me. How they never found that bullet. Pass right through him, right through his head. How can that be? One side to the other. How can a thing be moving that fast? And so small, you know, big as—no bigger than a—just so small. One side to the other. *(Pause.)* And he didn't make no sound. Only his arm flew up, hand hit me flat on the breast. Like that. Flat on my breast. *(Pause.)* On my breast. *(Pause.)* And then he went down. On the sidewalk. And you think, something like that happen, you think you in a dream. You do. You know, you can't take it as real. Everything stop for a minute. It seem everything stop. And it got so quiet after the shot, and it seem a long time. And I look down at him, and I think: what he doing? You know? What he doing down there? Even though I heard the shot, I didn't put it together. You hear that sound everyday. You know what it is. But you can't put that sound to your own child. You—you can't do it. And the blood: what is that? You know? What is that? And why his head look like that? For a time, seem like a long time, you try to make up some kinda story in your mind. Why his head look like that. Like there another meaning—how he look down there. That about something else. Not what it is. Like maybe he playing some kinda trick on me—somebody playing a trick on me. And you going through this in your mind. And it all seem like a long time, but then later on people tell you: no, you started screaming right after. But I know there was something in between. This in-between time. Before the knowledge. Before the truth. *(Pause.)* You know how they say time don't stop for no man. But sometime it do, I think. Or it slow down. Because I look down at him, and it was as if time got broken, the line of it got broken, and

I had to take a long step to get across from one second to the next. *(she is progressively becoming more upset)* And I get mad at myself sometimes, thinking: why I take that step? You know? Maybe I coulda walked over into some other idea. Walked over into some other story. You know, he trip, and that, that blood, it just, you know, his soda or something— cause he always carrying his little can. You know, why didn't I go there? Why didn't they let us go there? But, see, then you look up at everybody around you, and they all step back, and their hands up in the air, and their mouths open, and some other mother screaming—and it like they all telling you: go on, cross over, get to what it is. And then you look down again, and you see it. You see how the story go.

The Other Place

Sharr White

Dramatic
Juliana Smithton, early 50s

> *Juliana is speaking to Dr. Cindy Teller. She has begun coming to Dr. Teller because of an "episode" that Juliana suspects signifies brain cancer. Over the course of her evaluation, Juliana tells Dr. Teller about the disappearance, ten years ago, of her daughter, and of what Juliana now believes are her daughter's attempts to contact her.*

JULIANA: —Look, don't tell me sorry, that word exhausts me, I've heard that enough to never want to hear it again, but thank you, I know you're trying to be kind.

> *(Small beat.)*

I saw a photograph once, taken at the turn of last century; a man, Chinese man, attempts to assassinate the Emperor, they catch him, display him in a town square, sentence him literally to Death by a Thousand Cuts. They tie him to a scaffold, apply tourniquets to him, amputate his limbs a thousand times. Starting with his fingers and his toes. The photo shows him with about eight inches of each limb left and he's...gazing up into the sky with an...unspeakable look on his face. Something...beyond agony. Almost beatific. Like he is in such pain that he has transcended pain and is above himself watching himself experience his pain. Losing a child is like that.

> *(Small beat.)*

So then after years of walking around on my own private little scaffold, I get a call, a phone call. And ...it's her. Out of the blue. Believe it? See, this is what my husband says. Is it her, is it her, I tell him it's her, because it is her, my daughter is calling me. She calls and we have conversations. Short ones. But they are conversations. She and Richard are living somewhere, secretly, and they're married with two little girls. My phone rings, I answer it, there she is. I can hear the girls in the background. Sometimes I call her. All Ian can say is: Is it her. We're in negotiations. Where we can meet. She's jittery, probably a little embarrassed, but I'm not going to ask her any questions, not yet, I don't want to scare her off, I don't even know what name she goes by now, she could hang up and change her number and never call back and I would go through my thousand little deaths all over again. I want her to meet me at the other place. We have a house, my family house, my great-grandfather built it, on Cape Cod, we spent almost every weekend there, hell I've been there every weekend for almost my entire life, I could find it blindfolded from the bottom of the sea. I think I can get her to meet me there. I don't want to use the cancer as an excuse, but I do want her to know that … that it looks like time is …short. For me.

Pigmalion

Mark Dunn

Comic
Vicki, 20s

Poor Vicki Hill! This baby sister of the wealthy southern Hill family has watched long enough the undermining of her patrician family's reputation through their continual fraternizing with those far beneath them in the societal hierarchy. In this monologue, delivered to her far-more-accommodating sister Clara, Vicki waxes indignant on how far down her family has sunk in their societal standing as a result. She's absolutely (and rather obnoxiously) drawing the line at her brother Freddy getting romantically involved with the likes of ELiza Doolittle, impoverished pig farmer's daughter.

VICKI: Well, I was too late – at least for round one. I've had to postpone my chat with Freddy's new trailer-trash hussy girlfriend until *after* their first – and hopefully, *only* date. But she's still going to get an earful. I could care less who she is or *what* she is, but that girl has no right to intrude upon our family. To bring the shame of her deficient life into *our* lives. The same thing happened to Aunt Katherine, if you recall. She married that ex-wrestler and suddenly, one whole branch of our extended family became personas non grata. Snubbed by the Wimpole Garden Guild. No more invitations to the Cotton Factor's ball. I refuse to let this happen to us. No trash is coming into this house that isn't going to be promptly carried out in Hefty Bags by the maid. I realize that we've fallen a little short over the last few years, but I will not stand by and watch us all sink into the gutter. I plan to marry well, even if you do not. And no man of any importance in this town is going to cast even a glance in my direction while our brother chases after a pig farmer's daughter.

Rantoul and Die 1

Mark Roberts

Dramatic
Debbie, 40s

Debbie has had it with her husband, Rallis. Here, she tells him why.

DEBBIE: *(sighs)* Whoever you are, I don't love you. I don't believe I ever did. I remember walkin' up the aisle at our wedding, and the whole time I was thinkin', "I don't love this man...what am I doing?" But, I went through with it. And I lived with it. I thought this was maybe what life was supposed to be like. And I prayed that maybe as time passed I would grow to love you. But, it never kicked in. I just became more and more resentful of you. Every time you opened your mouth to talk, I'd have to turn away to keep from leaping at you and biting out your tongue. I'd lay in bed at night and look at the back of your head and I would imagine taking my pillow and smotherin' you. Knowing that life in prison had to be better than what I was livin'. You know, it does feel better to talk this stuff out. Ever since school you have been a stable guy. Decent job, decent car, you're half-way decent looking. And I had never been with a guy like you. I always warmed my hands over more rebellious creatures. But, that had it's own setbacks. Like a dislocated shoulder and three scrapes. So, when I met you, I thought, "Well, the rent will get paid and he probably won't hit me?" And both of those things were true. And I will always, and I mean this, I will always appreciate the way you treated me. You were sweet and considerate. But, I have to move on, because you are burying me alive. We have lousy sex, Rallis. Those rare times we do have it. It is the ugliest, clumsiest, unsexiest thing I have ever seen. And I used to work in a nursing home. We are not good as a couple. We gotta be strong. Don't get all babyish about it. Just move on to the next chapter in our lives. Remember Rallis, when one door closes a window usually opens. That's an Eastern thing.

(Beat.)

Now, you gonna sign them papers, or what?

Rantoul and Die 2

Mark Roberts

Seriocomic
Callie, 30s-40s

Callie is visiting Rallis, the soon-to-be ex-husband of a woman with whom Callie works at Dairy Queen. He has tried to off himself and is now incapacitated.

CALLIE: Anyway, the latest addition to our loving menagerie is "Tiny Louis". Although, the way he's been dominating the bowl lately, I don't think he's gonna be tiny that long. I found him skulking around the dumpster behind the DQ one night, and took him home. He brought the count up to fourteen. Which to me is a nice round number. Mother says we've gone overboard. But, I lovingly disagree. How can you have too many of something that gives you nothing but love? Not to say they don't every single one of them get into one of their moods once in a while. They do. But you just have to let them know who's boss. Like, the other night I was watching TV, and "Miss Gretchen" reared back on her hind legs and scratched me a real good one on my left calf. Just out of the blue. No provocation, whatsoever. Well, I snatched her up by her little neck and held her right in front of my face, and I said in a very stern voice, "Oh no you don't!" And she got it, believe you me. I don't like to get harsh with them, but you know, spare the rod, spoil the...cat. Most of the time they just love me up. I'll lay in bed at night reading, and I'll have thirteen cats laying all around me. "Bernard" likes to sleep with mother cause he can scratch his head on her bunions. But thirteen cats in one bed is plen-ty. It's about all the love I can handle. Sometimes I'll wake up in the middle of the night, and they'll all be purring. All thirteen of them, purring away. And it's like they'll get into a rhythm where they're all purring exactly the same way, at exactly the same time. The bed will actually start to move ever so slightly. And sometimes I'll pretend that I'm floating on a raft in the middle of the ocean. Only instead of water, it's a sea of cats. And they're keeping me afloat. It's soothing. I sometimes don't want to get out from under the covers, it's so peaceful. I love cats. But, I'll tell you what, come five-thirty every morning, each and every one of them is up and ready to have their breakfast. And they won't let me sleep. They'll start meowing and rubbing their heads on my face to wake me up. And when you got that many hungry cats you ain't gonna be able to ignore them. It becomes a mob mentality at that point.

(Smiles at Rallis)

Boy, you sure do love the DQ don't'cha? Well, it is the best soft serve around. I know a lot of people prefer custard, but they're wrong. I mean you know, to each his own I guess. I find it too sweet, personally. And I'm not saying that cause I'm the manager of the DQ. Even before I worked there, mom and I preferred their ice cream to the other stuff. I remember when I was little, every Saturday mom would say, "Callie, I believe you and I have earned us a Peanut Buster Parfait". And I'd take the five dollars and run over and grab us both a delicious frozen treat. Nothing better on a hot day. Am I right? I-am-right.

(Looks at Rallis)

Can I get you anything else? Well, you just let me know. Anything you want. If it ain't here, I'll go get it for you. I sure like talkin' to you, Rallis. Always have. Course, you're not too good at holding up your end of the conversation these days.

(Giggles)

Kidding, of course. I know you're brain-dead. Poor thing. But, at least it's better than dead-dead. Am I right? I do miss hearing the sound of your voice, though. Well, we just take what the Lord gives us and make the best of it. What else can you do? I trust in his Divine plan. I always have. I'm just happy knowing he's up there with his hand on the wheel, instead of leaving it up to us. And you gotta figure he has big plans for you, Rallis. I mean, you shoot yourself in the head, not once but twice, and he still doesn't let you die. You just know that he's going to use your life for some holy reason. Some heavenly lesson for the rest of us.

(Sighs, a beat)

Well, I better change that pee bag for you.

Running Amok

Quinn D. Eli

Comic
Daria, mid to late 30s

> *Daria, a successful sports agent, is perpetually over-caffeinated and passionately devoted to the Art of the Spin. Here she is talking to Al Bernstein, a reporter for ESPN, about her dearest client, a football player who is fending off rumors of an epic sex scandal.*

DARIA: *(on the phone)* No. Listen. Will you give the kid a break? ... I know that. I know how old he is, Al, I've been with him since the dawn of time, but I'm asking you to give him a break, okay? You wanna know why? How about outta simple human kindness, you son of a bitch, how about to be decent? You don't want to be on the wrong side of this thing, Al, this kid is a butterfly, do you hear me, and you're still treating him like a goddamn caterpillar ... if you print that shit, Al, we'll sue you, swear to god. That story is a lie...How do I know? You wanna know how I know? I've seen the girl's picture in the paper, that's how I know. She makes Lindsey Lohan look like Mother Theresa. If there was an Olympics for tramps, Al, she'd bring home the gold...If you were Catholic, Al, like me, you'd understand: scandal is everywhere, there's no escaping scandal, we live in a corrupt and morally depraved universe. But my guy's not some priest boffing altar boys, ok? My guy is the salt of the earth: he's married, he takes care of his parents, he gives to charity, for crissakes. And this girl you're quoting, Al, this April What's-Her-Name, she's a liar. The kid never had sex with her. Al... Al...Albert: last time I checked my copy of the Karma Sutra, a hand job in the dressing room at JC Penney does not constitute "sex"... Al, listen, my client says you've got it all wrong. ALL of it! First off, he was NEVER in JC Penney with that girl. Ever. If you print that he was in JC Penney with her, Al, swear to god, I'll make a charm bracelet outta your balls ... Good...excellent, thanks so much. Absolutely. He's a talented boy, Al, he's an inspiration to a lotta people. Little Johnny and Little Suzy, they look up to this kid—you don't wanna take that away. Thanks, Al, God bless.

A Russian Play

Don Nigro

Seriocomic
Irina, 40

In the summer of 1900, in the gazebo on the Russian estate of the Volkonsky family, Irina, an attractive widow, age 40, has just offered to marry Dr. Radetsky, a younger man who has actually been in love with all three of her daughters, and been rejected by him, and she's feeling sad and humiliated. All her life she's been the most beautiful woman in any room, and now, with her three lovely daughters, she is terrified that men won't look at her any more. She loves them, but she hates getting older, and losing her power over men. She is a bit scatterbrained but not at all unintelligent, with a sharp tongue and a sense of humor.

IRINA: A person gets a few lines in her face and she begins to understand desperation. The need for love really is a form of dementia. I miss my husband. I made him very unhappy, of course, but he loved his garden. He particularly loved the hedge-maze. It gave him so much pleasure. I could never understand why. It's always frightened me. I get lost in it. I've always gotten lost easily. It gets worse as I get older. But I've always been lost. The thing is, I panic. I get into the maze and I panic. I can't think straight. Of course, I've never been able to think straight. That's why I drink. To hide it. If I'm drinking all the time, people think that's why I can't think straight, but that's not the case. There is a deeper cause. There has always been this terrible whispering in my head. All these voices. But I can never quite make out what they're saying. And I don't think I actually want to know. It can't be anything good, can it? I'm so jealous of Katya. She's so smart. Her mind works like a German clock. Of course, intelligence doesn't make a person happy, but what does? I'm also jealous of Natasha, for her great beauty, and the depth of her passion. Natalya loves deeply. But she doesn't trust herself. And Anya. Anya is like a rosebud. She could flower into anything. But she's very fragile. I'm afraid to be near her. I'm terrified I'll say the wrong thing. I always say the wrong thing. Especially when I'm trying not to say the wrong thing. All my daughters hate me. It's not their fault, it's mine. I think I've done it on purpose. I regret it now, but it's too late to change it. And it's better that way. They loved their father so much, and look how miserable he made them when he died. When I'm gone, they'll be greatly relieved. That's my gift to my children. I've made it impossible for them to mourn my passing. You do believe that I was beautiful once, don't you? I have photographs.

Seven Minutes in Heaven

Steven Levenson

Dramatic
Phoebe, mid-teens

> *Phoebe is popular. A high school freshman, she's pretty and likeable and always perfectly upbeat. Underneath the surface, things are not so straightforward. She broke up with her boyfriend Hunter a few months ago to date Phil Marnell, but then she dumped Phil and now she and Hunter are sort of hooking up again, but all of a sudden she sort of almost misses Phil—it's complicated. Here, Phoebe talks about her childhood and the inner wounds that she has learned to cover up so convincingly.*

PHOEBE: Phil Marnell has a scar. It's tiny. You wouldn't even really see it unless you knew it was there and you were looking for it. It's from chicken pox and it's on his left temple and it's a little dot like somebody stamped him with a dot when he was born so that they would always be able to find him.

When I was ten, my dad quit his job so he could find out what he really wanted to do, and it started to look like what he really wanted to do was watch TV in his boxers and drink Diet Rite. My mom would come home at seven and I would be in my room and they would fight. My mom would yell and my dad would cry, and then my dad would yell and my mom would cry, and then my dad would curl up in a ball and rock himself back and forth and say the word, "please," over and over, until it didn't even sound like a word but more like a sound that an animal might make.

I used to sit in my closet on a pile of dirty clothes and push myself in against the door and I would wait for everything to stop. Sometimes my mom would leave and she wouldn't come back for a few hours. Or a few days. Sometimes my dad would say sorry and they would make up and we all had dinner together and Dad put pants on and everybody smiled, and those times were the worst. Sometimes I would sit there in the dark and I would imagine I wasn't really there or that somebody far away was dreaming me and what if they woke up. Sometimes I would take my fingernail and I would stretch it across my chest very slowly, so that the skin would begin to split and a little inch of blood would open into my shirt and then everything would get quiet and I didn't cry and I wasn't scared and I felt alone and emptied out and like maybe I would never die, but even if I did it would be ok.

(Beat.)

My dad would just keep saying, "please," until my mom left the room and then he would say, "love isn't free, Betsy. It costs you. It always costs you. It always costs you." It always costs you.

Seven Minutes in Heaven

Steven Levenson

Seriocomic
Margot, mid-teens

> *Margot, a high school freshman, is having a party at her house to introduce her friends to her out-of-town boyfriend, Mike. It's getting late and the party is winding down, but Mike remains a no-show. Margot is now stuck in "heaven," a claustrophobic basement closet with nerdy Wade, for seven minutes. She's already informed him that nothing is going to happen between them. To pass the time, Wade asks Margot what she thinks her life will be like after high school and college. As she speaks, the fantasy of her future unfolds before her.*

MARGOT: After college? Oh. We'll get married. It won't be a very big wedding. Just our family and our closest friends, on a beach somewhere. California maybe. My mom will cry the whole time. She'll be embarrassed afterwards when she looks at the pictures and her eyes are red and her make up is streaky. Mike will go to medical school and I'll go to law school. Afterwards Mike can start his own private practice. The worst part of his job will be telling a family bad news, and on days like that, he'll call me and I'll come home early and I'll hold him as tight as I can, and kiss him hard and say, look at me, Mike. Shh, Mike. Look at me. It's ok, Mike, you did everything you could do. I'll work at a firm just down the street from Mike's office, and some days, if we're not too busy, we'll meet up for lunch or just a cup of coffee or just to say hi. At night, we'll find little jars and fill them up with ten million fireflies. I'll hold my knees like this. Like I'm holding them right there. We'll go for a walk and he won't be late, and I'll act as normal as I can, and I'll wear his necklace until it breaks off and turns back into dirt and I won't say anything. You'll have three kids. Two of them will be yours, and then the last one you'll adopt. You'll name all of them after your favorite characters in your favorite books. You'll fill up jars with green apples and necklaces, and when you get old, you'll retire and put together all of your savings and buy a little cottage somewhere far away, where nothing else is, except for sheep and grass and the weather. You'll read books all day long and take walks for an hour on the last day, on Tuesday, the last day, and make fires in your fireplace and cook dinners from scratch and wait for your children and your grandchildren and your great-grandchildren to visit you. You'll have bony little fingers and the skin will hang off of your arms so you can see the blue veins underneath, like ropes. I'll have age spots on my hands and Mike's eyesight won't be great, and my arthritis will get worse, and then one morning, we won't wake up.

Things of Dry Hours

Naomi Wallace

Dramatic
Cali Hogan, 29, African-American.

1930's. Alabama. Night. Cali's father is asleep in his chair. Cali comes into the room in her nightgown. Tice stirs but does not wake. Cali quietly tears pages out of her father's large bible while she speaks.

CALI: Forgive me Father for I have sinned.
    (She tears out another page, but in short bursts so it tears differently)
Twice so far. Here goes a third.
    (She tears out a third page in a different manner from the other two)
That's a kinder music, Lord. He won't know it cause he only goes to his earmarked pages. When he wakes he won't be missin' somethin' he doesn't know he had. *(Beat.)* And I need it to wipe 'cause he won't let me use the party newspaper. *(She puts the torn pages into her pocket, then stands over her father)* I'm goin' to bed. You still asleep? *(She lightly brushes his hair once, but doesn't want to wake him.)* Still a handsome man. But I can't remember her like you do cause I was only six but she must of loved you up 'til you couldn't stand it anymore. Because you never seemed to need to find it again. What was it like, Daddy, to be loved like that? I lied to you. My husband's eyes are not open in his grave. They were closed when he lived and closed when he died. He never could bear to look at me. I mean, really look at me. You ever have a hand touch you like it was touchin' a table, or reachin' for a bowl of soup? Then you'd know me

This

Melissa James Gibson

Dramatic
Jane, 38

Jane is at a party at some friends' house. She is disabusing them of the notion that she had the perfect marriage. She is a little drunk.

JANE: Our Marriage was not Perfect.
    I don't know why people insist on
        clinging to this fiction
    Sure Roy was a Great Guy but ours
        was a Regular Marriage
    We had Ups we had Downs most
        recently we were in a Down but
    he got sick so it never did have a
        chance to fall apart and maybe it
        never would have fallen apart but
        we'll never know and I got all the glory
    I wanted to tell people I Don't Warrant
        Your Commiseration
    But without my having done anything
        to deserve it my stock went up after
        I became a widow
    And surviving spouses become blank slates
        onto which those around them project
        this
    this Tragic Sheen they secretly hope
        their own deaths will one day engender
    And people can become extremely Entitled
        when it comes to their commiseration
        and can be extremely Forceful in their
        efforts to make you accept it
    Really people have such tiresome
        fantasies about the dead
    They romanticize final conversations
    They become exhilarated by their own grief
    They feel a sudden compulsion to belong to

the inner circle of the dead person's
ex-life
It's bizarre
People started talking about Roy like
he was Desmond fucking Tutu and
you know what He wasn't Desmond fucking Tutu
He was just a Regular Great Guy who we
all wish didn't die 50 years prematurely
Why can't that be enough

This

Melissa James Gibson

Dramatic
Jane, 38

Jane is outside her 10 year-old daughter Maude's door, trying to get her to unlock it and trying to apologize for the way things have been since Maude's daddy died.

Jane: A person needs to eat Maude
even when she's angry
especially when she's angry Anger takes
a lot of energy so if you want to stay really mad Maude
You Need To Eat
  (Sticking her finger on the plate of food)
It's cold now I'm sorry
I'm so sorry Maude
I don't know what else to say
Mommy screwed up
  (Knocking on the door)
Will you let me in
Will you
just let me know that you hear me please
Slam on the wall or
something Maude
  (No response. Standing up)
You know what this has gone on long enough
I need to check on you Maude I'm
opening this door Maude Mommy's
coming in
  (Opening the door to Maude's room)
Oh are you
asleep
  (Entering the room)
You are
asleep
  (Pause.)
I'm sorry you went to sleep angry

And hungry
I'm sorry I've been somewhere else
for the past year
I'm sorry for all the questions I couldn't
answer
About geography and the Aurora
Borealis
I'm sorry for so many things
I'm sorry for
the lullaby I sang to you when you
were a baby
You remember
the one entitled
For Fuck's Sake Go To Sleep
I meant it
in a good way
I'm sorry for
the time when you were in second grade and didn't proofread your
homework and I said you hadn't paid attention to capitalization and you
said you were done with your homework and done with capitalization
and I said
in this horrible and highly charged tone of voice I said
WELL IT'S YOUR LIFE
I'm sorry for all the times I used you
as an excuse to extract myself from
situations in which I didn't want to
participate
I'm sorry for your computational challenges
your flat feet
your future osteoporosis
your propensity toward nail-biting
the strange length of your arms and your
irredeemable sweet tooth
You come by all of it honestly and
genetically
    (Pause)
The night your father died I had a
fleeting thought
that went something like
Oh Okay Now I'll be allowed to have

sex with a couple more people before
I die
but I
didn't mean This
    (Pause)
Why did your father die Maude
Why die
Why die
Don't die Maude
Don't Do It
Ever
Oh that's selfish of me
I don't mean to put that kind of
pressure on you I mean
do what you need to do but
try Really Hard not to die Maude
please because
That
I could not bear
    (Picking up a carrot from Maude's tray and taking a bite)
Okay
I'm here now Maude
I'm back

Time Stands Still

Donald Margulies

Dramatic
Sarah, late-30s

Sarah is a photojournalist who has recently returned from Iraq, where she was injured by an I.E.D. which killed her translator (and, it turns out, her lover). She is speaking to the young wife of her photo editor, who doesn't understand why she does what she does, about a suicide bombing she witnesses and photographed.

SARAH: I had a flashback. Market bombing. Mosul. Couple of years ago. I'm shooting these women. The inmates. With the babies they'd had in prison. And some of these ladies are seriously bad. I mean, homicide; drug dealing, trying to kill their grandmother for her ATM card, that kind of thing... Anyway I'm shooting... sort of getting in the zone and this one woman... big... heavily tattooed with Hell's Angels-kind of skulls with fire shooting out of the eye sockets, comes up to me, gets right in my face... and looks at me with such... contempt... *(Brutish voice)* "What you want to take my picture for? Huh?" And... I was back in Mosul. You were off doing a story in the south; it was when I was there for the AP. I never told you. I never told anybody. The light that day was gorgeous, I remember.

(Pause.)

I was sitting in a cafe with the Reuters guys... And a car bomb went off, a block or two away, in this market. And I just ran to it, took off. Without even thinking. *(A beat.)* The carnage was... ridiculous. Exploded produce. Body parts. Eggplants. Women keening. They were digging in the rubble for their children. I started shooting. And suddenly this woman burst out from the smoke... covered in blood... her skin was raw and red and charred, and her hair was singed - she got so close I could smell it - and her clothes, her top had melted into her, and she was screaming at me.

(shouts)

"Go way, go way! No picture, no picture!" And she started pushing me, pushing my camera with her hand on the lens...I kept on shooting. Then, somehow, I ran the hell out of there. I stopped to catch my breath... and check out my cameras...

(Pause.)

There was blood on my lens. *(Moved)* Her blood was smeared on my lens.
  (She breaks down.)
I feel so ashamed...What I did was so wrong. It was indecent. They
didn't want me there! They did not want me taking pictures! They lost
children in that mess! To them it was a sacred place. But there I was, like
a, like some kind of ghoul with a camera shooting away. No wonder
they wanted to kill me; I would've wanted to kill me, too. I live off the
suffering of strangers. I built a career on the sorrows of people I don't
know and will never see again.

Tomorrowland

Neena Beber

Seriocomic
Anna, 20s-30s

Anna is the head writer of a TV series about a prepubescent girl. Here she is talking to her producer, Wyatt, about a surreal vision she has had involving Disney World.

ANNA: So I'll go to the mall. I'll drive to the mall and I'll get lost five times, I'll keep ending up on the road to Disneyworld, I'll turn around but there's a loop, a magical loop that sucks me back every time. Then suddenly there it is, enormous, windowless, surrounded by parked cars. Right in the middle of nowhere. A million cars parked in the middle of nowhere. The mall is huge. I'll never find the others, it's huge. I buy a bar of violet-colored soap. I buy a denim shirt for half-price identical to the one I already have but the new one looks older, more worn. I buy a jar of hand cream that smells like vanilla wafers, I think it will make a nice gift for someone, I keep it for myself. I buy three pairs of socks in different shades of green because I can't decide which one and they are all lovely, they all fill me with desire. I give them money and they give me things, salespeople with good skin and white teeth. A simple transaction. Perfect and pure. When I get back to the car I take out my loot on the seat next to me and look at it. Then I wrap it up again. Perfect and pure, perfect and pure, when the feeling goes I'm empty again I am empty I HAD ALL KINDS OF PLANS ONCE, I HAD PLANS, I am empty. I don't know where I am. I drive without asking for directions. I think it will turn up, a sign, any sign I'll recognize but I get lost again. I'm lost. I got lost again. I'm really, really sick of getting lost. I must have made a wrong turn. It's impossible to read the signs properly. There was a sign with two arrows pointing in two different directions. What does that mean? I can't understand any of the arrows, they're all very ambiguous if you ask me. I ended up in this giant empty parking lot. At least it looked like an empty parking lot. Then again, everything around here looks like an empty parking lot. A guard in this van drove over to me flashing his red light, told me I was in the place where they make missiles. Usually when I get lost, I get sucked into Disneyworld. And there's nothing here. There's nothing, nothing here. The restaurants are all...they all have themes.

Pirates, Castles, even sushi is Sushi World, papier mache. The kite store...
the kite store in the park? I went to buy one. I thought I would buy a kite,
I'll fly a kite, I'll do that. I saw kites in the window, I went inside to buy
one but there was no inside. It's just a window. A fake store window of a
fake kite store in a fake Ghirardelli Square in a fake-- I'm losing it, Wyatt.

The Trial of Mata Hari
Elaine Kendall

Dramatic
Mata Hari, 40

> *"Mata Hari" was the stage name of Margaretha Geertruida "Grietje" Zelle MacLeod, a Dutch exotic dancer, courtesan, and accused spy. She was 40 years old at the time of her trial, charged with spying for Germany during the First World War. Here, she is speaking to the military tribunal that found her guilty of all espionage charges, sentencing her to execution by firing squad. Mata Hari was executed the following day, October 15, 1917.*

MATA HARI: I will speak for myself. I am absolutely innocent of these charges! To the first charge, I answer that I was in Paris in December 1915, on a government-approved visa. To the second and third charges, I swear I did not give documents or information to Consul Karl Kroemer while I was in the Hague in 1916. To the third charge, I admit I met with Consul Karl Kroemer on another occasion, but gave him no information of any kind. I had none. To the fourth charge, I returned to Paris in June of 1916 only because I love the country and the city above all others, and wished to live there. Until this moment, I believed that love was returned. To the fifth charge, I did not maintain contact with Germans during my stay in the Paris in 1916. The two policemen sent by Captain Ladoux to follow me every moment of the day and report to him found nothing remotely incriminating either in my activities or my possessions. Both of those officers gave sworn testimony to that fact. Believe them, if you refuse to believe me! To the sixth charge: I became acquainted with Major Kalle in Madrid in December 1916 because Captain had sent me there to ingratiate myself with German officials. Those meetings with Kalle were in service of France. As God is my witness, I swear it! To the seventh charge, I answer that never did I pass documents that might damage the operations of the French army or endanger the security of military establishments. I had no such documents nor any information about interior politics, the spring offensive, or the French discovery of the secret of German invisible ink. In November 1916, when I was aboard the Hollandia bound for my home in the Netherlands, the ship's captain told me that a Belgian couple on the ship were spies. To your eighth charge, I swear that I never met with Germans in Paris in January

1917. I was under surveillance the entire time, and no such meetings, telephone calls, or messages were ever reported. None. I beg you to let me speak the truth in my own defense. I am not French. I have the right to have friends in other countries, even those at war with France. I am a Dutch citizen, and Holland is neutral. I love France, and count on the good hearts of French officers to find me innocent of these charges I have loved and been loved by French officers and private citizens, and cannot understand why they have all united against me. You have heard Prosecutor Mornet say that what I have done is unbelievable! I implore you, officers of the tribunal, to accept the fact that it is...unbelievable!

Until We Find Each Other

Brooke Berman

Seriocomic
Sophy, 33

> *Sophy was a retired stripper and Orthodox Jew. Now, she's a ghost. She speaks to the audience, welcoming them into the play.*

SOPHY: Welcome Ye of the Congregation of the Broken Hearted. Welcome Motherless Children. Welcome you who wrestle with Angels. I used to wrestle with angels too. But not anymore.

I, Mistress Sophy, am the Spiritual Leader of the Congregation of the Broken Hearted, Musical Director of the Chorus of Falling Angels. Usher of the coming times, the world that is to come, constantly constantly constantly coming..... I know about constantly coming. And I bet you'd like to, huh? Want me to share? Because for a limited time only, for a drink and a good meal, for fifty bucks, maybe a hundred (cause rates are going up) I'll tell you what I see and what I know. I'll look into your soul and tell you what I pick up. Want that? Fifty bucks to look at your soul, a hundred and I'll throw in a blowjob. No, I'm just kidding. I don't do that anymore.

Hey, I could be Elijah for all you know. Capitalism makes everyone a whore.

Maybe just maybe... I'm gonna tell you some secrets. For getting found. Cause getting lost is a thing of the past. And now we're all getting found.

Until We Find Each Other

Brooke Berman

Seriocomic
Sophy, 33

Sophy was a retired stripper and Orthodox Jew. Now, she's a ghost. Here, she speaks to the audience.

SOPHY: This is the best part. How I Met Him.

Okay, so to start with, here's me, eighteen, tripping, barefoot, in college, at the Student Union, I was always surprised that no one seemed to notice, I mean, I still got good grades and -- so, here's me, barefoot and dancing and high, stealing muffins from the cafeteria -- I finally got out of the house, that one I grew up in, but for what? I mean, I thought I'd leave home and this whole shining life would be there waiting for me, and The Shining Life would say "Thank you for your great courage, for surviving that mess of a family. Thank You -- for getting out. No one ever believed you and no one ever stopped the bad things from happening and no one heard you scream, but Good Girl Good Girl Good GOOD GOOD GOOD how you got yourself out. We, your Shining Life Guardian Angels, have been waiting for you... here's your good girl new life, waiting" Only it wasn't like that at all. Nobody took me in their arms. And nothing was waiting. And my mother still called me in the middle of the night drunk and both of them, my parents, even expected me to come home on vacations and act like a perfect, normal suburban girl only I'd get thrown out if I showed up discernably high or if they found anything on me, so okay, I got thrown out a lot. I mean, a lot. Til I left forever.

And then, I met them, my rabbi and his wife. Someone brought me, and there I was. At the Student Union. Union of students. In Union. Barefoot and high. With a group of Jews. I don't remember too much else about it. But I think it saved my life. The union of the students, and him. I dropped out of school and studied and gathered and celebrated and ate and I met that musician and we moved to Israel, made aliyat, and then I left his ratty ass and came back again, single, broke and disowned. But never happier.

And even when I danced, for money, even when I left the community, or went back, or was poor and making big mistakes, I made mistakes -- I always had Hashem. I was never lost.

The world makes you think there's something in between YOU and where your soul comes from. But what if there isn't? What if there isn't? Come on, Sweet One. Ye of Little Faith. Come on, come on, come on, come on...

Venus Flytrap

Anthony Dodge

Comic
Butch Diamond, 20-30

Some people pose tough, some people are tough only when they feel like it, but Butch Diamond has the kind of toughness forged through years of hardship. A private detective, Butch has been on her own for many years. Butch had a number of restless years, not in terms of her sexuality--removed from the clutches of her parents was liberating--Diamond's struggle is determining her place in society, finding work and fulfillment in it. Being a detective was part of it, her clientele the rest of the equation--she could help the misfits who have no one to help them. Diamond is attractive, smart and determined. Here, at the start of the play, Butch is talking to the audience in the great tradition of the film noir voiceover.

DIAMOND: Pearl Harbor isn't just the name of a drag queen at the Klub Kockadero. Nope, December 7th, 1941 changed everything--the boys went to war and left us girls in charge. They've rationed the whole shebang from gasoline to nylon stockings, and there's a shortage of nearly everything including dick.

(Takes a big hit on her smoke. Lets it out slowly.)

I'm talking about private dick. That's me: a shamus, a gumshoe, a private eye. The name's Diamond. Butch Diamond. The private dick without one. Since I'm fast on my feet and good with my dukes I've side stepped into the detective business. It's a way to make a buck for now, and with the fellas slugging it out with Tojo, or mixing it up with Adolph "Over There", it's easy over here for an enterprising doll like me to finagle work. Some of it honest. Sin isn't just in our nature, it's our legacy from God— and She is one tough old broad. Even though we're at war, Mr. & Mrs. America keep committing the same old crimes ever since Adam and his moll Eve and The Case of the Stolen Apple. People keep on hurting each other, stealing from each other, killing each other. For that there's no shortage.

(Drops her smoke to the ground and rubs it out with the toe of her shoe.)

I'm not grumbling. It's good for business. Dunno know how long I'll stick with it, guess I'll play it a few times more and see if I like the tune.

(She adjusts her brim, flips up her collar.)

In case you're not a detective, I'm what some might call a lesbian; a Dyke Dick. Just not to my face. Don't get me wrong, I'm no man-hater or anything like that--you never know when you might need one to walk the dog or open ajar of pickles. I just don't have much use for one personally. I remember when I was a little baby Butch; my Daddy had me in our kitchen up on the counter top. He was standing close in front of me, smiling that smile of his. That smile that I always tried to make happen and never could. "Little Sister, he sez,"he always called me Little Sister—"Little Sister, I'll catch you. Daddy'll catch you." So I gave a smile back and did a Swan Dive off the counter.

(Indicates a high dive heading south with a descending whistle punctuated with a "splat!")

Landed face down on the linoleum. Then Dad sez: "Let that be a lesson to you, Little Sister--You can't trust nobody." So, I don't. And for a private eye, it makes swell sense not to. You may wonder what kinda mugs need a defective detective like me. Pretty much the same old song: either you're trying to get the goods on someone or someone is trying to get the goods on you. But there are those who don't fit in a little cubbyhole--hookers, junkies, "On sexual deviants —my crowd. Disaffected souls you won't find behind a white picket fence the Sunny Side of the Street," but still in need of someone to offer a little brains or a little muscle. Usually both.

We Are Here

Tracy Thorne

Dramatic
Billie, 32

Billie is speaking to her husband, Hal. Billie and Hal's son, Eli, has died after a long illness. Hal has been encouraging Billie to move on, perhaps by helping others in a similar situation, but Billie is trying to hold onto her boy by holding onto her grief.

BILLIE: Here I am thinking I'm a big shot for not getting in your way. For actually staying out of your way! Even for digging out my tattered, 'power of positive thinking' from the olden days. Sure, I realize Mother Theresa would step in and run the whole show but, since my limitations are obvious, I've been patting myself on the back that I didn't jump out the window when you first talked about it! It's a fine thing, Hal. Feel great about yourself, you're on the fast track to sainthood. Oh sugar, I don't blame you. How could I, it never crossed my mind either! Never occurred to me that the force of my will, since I was handed such a shitload of it, wouldn't be enough. Can you believe it?! SHAWN'S BEEN RIGHT ALL ALONG! Nobody gets to decide nothing! Nobody earns a happy life! If you happen to have one–it's just an accident! A 'happy' accident! Now, that works better for you, doesn't it? What a shame and who cares anyway, right?! My real point is--if you don't know how to help me, neither do you know how to help yourself and I, sure as anything, have left you high and dry in that department. You've embraced your misery for years, dined out on it even, it's what makes you so charming, Eeyore. But you can't do the same with your grief, can you? So your foundation. Is a perfect distraction. A noble distraction from your grief. But here's a problem. I don't want to be distracted from my grief. My grief is all that's left. It's the only pulse the kid's got. And you want to talk about unfathomable? What's unfathomable to me is that there's no measure of it. There is no bottom. No outside edge. No dimension of any kind. My grief is everything to me. So you want to help somebody with something? Go ahead. See if you can help that.

Where the Great Ones Run

Mark Roberts

Seriocomic
Kylie Pound, mid-30s

> *Kylie, a waitress in a dusty Indiana truck stop, has a brightly made-up face,*
> *an ample bust line, and a vibrant emotionality. Her boyfriend Owen, on the*
> *other hand, is smallish, odd-looking, and suffers from a stutter that he's had*
> *since childhood. Near the end of the play, Kylie tells a fellow waitress that she*
> *has decided to marry Owen, despite having locked him out of her apartment*
> *just the day before.*

KYLIE: I realize it's out of the blue. It's certainly not the way I saw it playin'
out. But, last night, he and I went to the stock car races at the fair. By
the way, you know what they have there now? Deep-fried Snickers bars.
Yes. They take a Snickers bar, dip it in batter, and toss that thing in the
deep fryer. Very decadent. And yes, truly delicious. I'll be back on my
diet the day after tomorrow. Anyway, we're at the stock car races, and I
don't really care for them. Loud, and the people that go to them are ...
I don't wanna say stupid ... but, not my tribe. Anyway, I'm bored out
of my mind, and at a certain point I look over at Owen. And he's just
enthralled with these things. Just cars crashin' into each other and the
man is transfixed. And I stare at him, he doesn't know I am. He's sippin'
a beer, watchin' the cars. Sippin' the beer, watchin' the cars. And he's
smiling like a little kid. Looked like a litde boy sittin' there. And I started
imagining him as a little boy, and thought how happy his folks must've
been when he was born. And I started thinkin' of him gain' to school
and the other kids makin' f-f-f-fun of him. And how hard that must've
been. And I felt my heart just ache for that poor pitiful little boy. And
then I started feelin' a kind of affection for him. And then I started to
think that I wanted to be the person to love him. To take care of him.
To try and make his life a little better. I mean, I think you decide who
you wanna love. And I've decided I want to love him

SCENES

After the Revolution

Amy Herzog

Dramatic
Emma, 26
Jess, 28

> *Emma runs a foundation named for her grandfather, who was blacklisted during the McCarthy era. Here, her sister Jess tells her that, in fact, their grandfather was a spy for the Russians.*

(Emma and Jess in Jess's small apartment.)

JESS: And he's cool about working for you?

EMMA: What do you mean?

JESS: A lot of guys couldn't handle that.

EMMA: He's a feminist.

JESS: Yeah, he's dating you, it goes without saying he's a feminist, but...

EMMA: What?

JESS: N o, if it's working, it's working. I mean, I would not want to be your employee, I give him a lot of credit.

EMMA: What about you? New man in your life?

JESS: No, my year's not quite up yet.

EMMA: Your----?

JESS: Oh. You're not supposed to date anyone until you've been out for at least a year.

EMMA: Oh. Oh.

JESS: No need to be embarrassed.

(Emma shakes her head.)

EMMA: I'm not.

JESS: You are, but it's cool.

(Brief pause)

Mel said your speech was incredible.

EMMA: You talked to Mel?

JESS: We talk on Sundays. Sometimes dad gets on the phone, if he's not feeling too emotionally fragile. Which he was this week.

EMMA: Are you serious? He won't get on the phone with you?

JESS: Not out of malice, he just – you know him, he gets upset.

EMMA: I just think that's incredibly fucked up.

JESS: Whoa, negative words about our father?

EMMA: I'm shocked.

JESS: Well. It's not like you're calling me every Sunday, sis.

EMMA: I'm sorry.

JESS: Yeah, let's not do that, I'm just making the point that it can be a challenge to have an addict in the family, I'm done throwing the blame around.

EMMA: *(the sarcasm slips out)*

That's clear.

(Brief pause)

JESS: What?

EMMA: So I actually need to tell you something.

JESS: Yeah, I thought it was a long trip just for a visit.

EMMA: This going to be really hard. But I was very hurt that no one told me, and I made it a priority to come tell you in person.

JESS: Okay. I'm listening.

EMMA: Grandpa Joe spied for the Russians during World War II.

(Pause. No discernible reaction from Jess)

JESS: I'm just thinking about how to respond to this.

EMMA: I know. I know.

JESS: N o, um. I don't think you do. Actually. Sweetie, I already knew that. Should I not have told you that?

EMMA: *(forced calm)*

How did you know?

JESS: Dad told me.

(Brief pause)

EMMA: When?

JESS: When? Um. Three? No four. Four? Years ago?

EMMA: Four years ago?

JESS: It was right after the first time I got out of rehab, so that was...ninety--five. Yeah, about four years ago.

EMMA: How did it.../come up?

JESS: Funny story, actually. It was when took me on that trip to London, that 'you got out of rehab' reward, penitent--father--fucked--up--daughter--bonding--type--thing. And while we were there he took me to Marx's grave. Not first on my list of tourist attractions but also not up for debate. And he started crying. Which I found to be over the top. I asked him what was wrong, and that's when he told me.

EMMA: H e said grandpa was a spy.

JESS: That was the gist of it. And I was kind of like, I appreciate your sharing this huge thing with me, but we both know the real reason you're crying is that I'm such a colossal disappointment so let's not dress it up, you know?

EMMA: 1995 was the year I started the Joe Joseph fund.

JESS: Okay.

EMMA: It just seems like it might have come up.

JESS: I was back in rehab three weeks later, so it wasn't strictly speaking my tip-top priority.

EMMA: Well I guess that's the end of the conversation.

JESS: What does that mean?

EMMA: That's how you avoid every tough subject, that's how you recuse yourself from being part of our family, I'm not sure if you're aware of that.

JESS: He specifically asked me not to tell you. That's why I didn't say anything. I'm sorry you put me in a position where I had to tell you that.
(Brief pause)
You know in group I talk about you a lot. About how I feel bad that you didn't really get to have a childhood, fucked up as I was.

EMMA: I'm sorry, but I'm not sure what the right response is to that. Is it thank you?
(pause. Jess takes this with some grace.)

JESS: Are you staying with Dad and Mel, while you're up here?

EMMA: No. With Uncle Leo.

JESS: Can I give you one tiny piece of advice? Punishing dad isn't as fun or satisfying as you think it's going to be.

EMMA: I'm not punishing him.

JESS: Okay.

EMMA: I'm trying to surround the situation.

JESS: Well go easy on him.

EMMA: Are you serious?

JESS: The irony is not lost on me. Just some hard won wisdom, or whatever.
(Brief pause)
You gonna be okay?

EMMA: Am I gonna be okay?

JESS: Um. Yeah.
(they look at each other. End scene.)

Collapse

Allison Moore

Seriocomic
Hannah, mid 30's. Slightly uptight.
Susan, mid-30s. A chaos magnet.

We are in Hannah's condo. It is morning, and Hannah is getting ready for work. Her sister arrived the night before after losing her job and her apartment in LA. While Hannah was out last night searching for a PTSD support group for her husband, David, David and Susan stayed back at the condo getting drunk. Unbeknownst to Hannah, Susan has involved David in the delivery of an illicit package.

(The condo. It is the next morning. Hannah is almost dressed for work. Susan is in her pajamas.)

HANNAH: Susan, just tell me where David went.

SUSAN: He's running an errand.

HANNAH: What kind of errand?

SUSAN: He didn't really say.

HANNAH: Did he say anything about an appointment?

SUSAN: What appointment?

HANNAH: His doctor's appointment, at nine?

SUSAN: Ooo.

HANNAH: What?

SUSAN: Nothing.

HANNAH: Okay. You know what? That's fine. He is a grown man, he knows when the appointment is. And I have to go to work now. That is all I can control.

SUSAN: Okay.

HANNAH: I mean, I'm not going to track him down and physically drag him to the appointment to make sure he gets there, am I? No. So I have to let it go. I have to admit I am powerless, and trust that David will remember that he has a very important appointment at nine, and that he will be there. And if you see him, and you feel like reminding him about the appointment, I would appreciate that. But again, that is not anything I can control.

SUSAN: Thank God. I thought you were gonna freak when you figured out he's been gone since ten-thirty.

HANNAH: But it's—wait, you're saying he's been gone since ten-thirty last night?

(Hannah runs to the office.)

SUSAN: I want to stress that none of this is my fault.

(Hannah re-enters.)

HANNAH: The aero bed hasn't been slept in.

SUSAN: I know.

HANNAH: When I came home last night, you said he was asleep, in the office, on the aero bed.

SUSAN: He told me not to tell you he was gone.

HANNAH: He's been missing since last night?!

SUSAN: He is not missing, Hannah. You just don't know where he is.

HANNAH: Jesus Christ.

(Hannah dials her phone.)

SUSAN: I also feel the need to point out that you were very quick to believe he was sleeping on the aero bed. One might even say you seemed relieved you wouldn't have to deal with him when you traipsed in at one in the morning.

HANNAH: *(leaving a message)*

David, honey, call me as soon as you get this, okay?

SUSAN: It must have been quite the 'gathering.' Meet some interesting people?

HANNAH: You should have told me David was gone last night.

SUSAN: It wasn't my choice to be pushed into the middle of your marital subterfuge.

HANNAH: There is no subterfuge! My husband has been gone all night, no one knows where he is-

SUSAN: Maybe being gone all night is a good thing, did you think of that?

HANNAH: He has PTSD, Susan. He could be having a flashback or something!

(Beat.)

SUSAN: All right, look. He told me not to tell you, but: David is on a mission.

HANNAH: A what?

SUSAN: A mission.

HANNAH: What kind of mission?

SUSAN: This is a good thing, Hannah! He's embracing his fears.

HANNAH: Oh dear God.

SUSAN: I mean, technically, it was my mission.

HANNAH: What?

SUSAN: But not cosmically, because it became so clear that David should do it.

HANNAH: Okay, I'm gonna ask you this once, and I don't want any bullshit: what, exactly, is the mission? An expectation.

SUSAN: Being completely broke, unemployed, and newly homeless, I agreed to deliver a package to a man here called "Bulldog" in exchange for my plane ticket.

HANNAH: What.

SUSAN: I had no other choice, Hannah. Not all of us can be perfect.

HANNAH: Did you say his name is "Bulldog?"

SUSAN: Well I don't think that's his real name, but I don't know. I don't even know what's in the package. But see, obviously, there was a bigger plan at work, because when Bulldog called last night, David answered the phone-

HANNAH: No!

SUSAN: Yes! And David just took control, Hannah. He arranged a time for the "drop" and then said he was going to get some supplies and "scope out the site"-

HANNAH: What time did he, what time did "Bulldog" call?

SUSAN: I don't really remember-

HANNAH: WHAT TIME WAS IT?

SUSAN: Nine-thirty?

HANNAH: Jesus Christ. It's him.

SUSAN: Who?

HANNAH: Bulldog! Oh my God.

HANNAH: digs through her purse, pulls out a napkin, starts dialing a number on her phone.

SUSAN: See! This is proof that—wait, how do you know Bulldog?

HANNAH: What time is David supposed to meet him?

SUSAN: Eight o'clock, by the river at Gold Medal Park. Maybe this is your mission.

HANNAH: *(leaving a message)*

Hi, Bulldog. It's Hannah. *(I guess you know my name now. That was stupid.)* All right, look, I don't know what kind of game you're running, and if you planned everything last night or if this is just the mother of all coincidences. But I know all about your meeting this morning at Gold Medal Park. And I am on my way there, right now. I know you talked to David on the phone, but he does NOT have what you want. He does not have your, your-

SUSAN: "Package"-

HANNAH: Your "package." I have your package. I'm the only one you talk to, is that clear? I am leaving right now. I will be there in fifteen minutes, tops. Do not go into the park. I repeat, do not go into the park. I will meet you at the entrance, at the corner of Second and Portland. And just remember, I know how to find you. So be there.

(Hannah hangs up.)

SUSAN: Oh my God-

HANNAH: Get your jacket.

SUSAN: You're fucking Bulldog.

HANNAH: No!

SUSAN: Then what was that all about?

HANNAH: I met him at the meeting, all right? While you and David were shot-gunning beers and engaging in interstate trafficking, I went to find a PTSD support group!

SUSAN: Don't blame your affair on me, Hannah.

HANNAH: How about the part where you involve David in illegal activity and then lie to me about it, can I blame you for that?

SUSAN: I have boundary issues, I was adopted.

HANNAH: We were both adopted!

SUSAN: Maybe that's why you're fucking Bulldog.

HANNAH: Okay, it's seven-forty-two. We're going down to the park now. You are gonna find David, and I am gonna deal with Bull— with Ted. All right?

SUSAN: No wonder he goes by Bulldog.

HANNAH: We are gonna get this all taken care of by eight-forty-five so David can get down to Dr. Greenwood's office to jack off into a little cup, and I can get to my deposition at nine for the one client I've managed to land in the past six months and then go be impregnated.

SUSAN: What about the package?

HANNAH: I'll handle it, all right? You just find David.

SUSAN: Okay.

HANNAH: Oh my God. Gold Medal Park is—it's right by the bridge.

The Dew Point

Neena Beber

Seriocomic
Greta, 20s
Mimi, 30s

Greta, a young woman dating Jack, the former boyfriend of Mimi, stops by Mimi's home unannounced when she suspects that Mimi and Jack are still seeing each other. Mimi, who is ten years Greta's elder, spars with Greta about whether or not it is possible to remain good friends with ex-lovers.

(Mimi is settling down to work. A light tapping at the door. She doesn't hear it as she finishes a mug of tea, goes to her desk. The tapping grows louder and more rhythmic. She looks through the peephole.)

MIMI: Hello? Oh.

(Mimi opens the door, Greta enters.)

GRETA: Hi.

MIMI: Greta.

GRETA: Sorry I didn't call first.

(Mimi looks at her, waiting. An awkward pause.)

Can I have something to drink?

MIMI: Sure. A glass of water?

(pointedly)

Milk?

GRETA: Do you have orange juice?

MIMI: We might.

(Mimi starts for the kitchen.)

GRETA: "We might." That's nice. To be able to say that.

MIMI: What?

GRETA: That must be nice, to be a "we."

MIMI: Just orange juice, then?

GRETA: Yeah. Just juice.

(Mimi exits to the kitchen. Greta looks around. Picks up a photo or two. Picks up the cassette tape, reads the label, puts it back down. Sees the chair. Sits on it. Mimi comes back with a half-full glass of orange juice.)

MIMI: This is all we have left. I have left.

GRETA: Thanks. I'm addicted to orange juice. I fucking love it lately. I don't know why that is. I go through these phases, like sometimes, sometimes

I just need to have this particular ingredient, for like, weeks. I was on yogurt for a while. I was on bologna for an entire month. Bologna sandwiches. I just had to have 'em. And I'm a vegetarian.

(Mimi looks at her, not sure what to say.)

MIMI: I'm actually about to get to work, I've got a ton to do today so--

GRETA: This is Jack's chair.

MIMI: He made it, yes.

(pause)

GRETA: It's not very comfortable.

(tiny pause)

MIMI: Kai doesn't think so, either. It was an engagement present. Kai is my— the one to whom I am engaged.

GRETA: This is a nice place.

MIMI: Thank you.

GRETA: I like the way you've got it.

MIMI: Thanks. It's still kind of hodge-podge, but, you know.

GRETA: You've got nice stuff.

(pause)

MIMI: So what's up, Greta?

GRETA: Is it mostly yours or his?

MIMI: It's both of ours. It's a mixture. We got some of it together.

GRETA: You work at home?

MIMI: Yes, Greta, which is why it's kind of difficult to begin my day sometimes so if you'll please--

GRETA: Why am I here?

MIMI: It's nice to see you, but I'm trying to get to work, actually, so yes, perhaps—you should tell me, yes, the reason you came here. I want to know the truth.

MIMI: The truth?

GRETA: I want to know. Are you sleeping with Jack?

MIMI: Am I what?

GRETA: I have a right to know.

MIMI: Jesus.

GRETA: What is going on between the two of you?

MIMI: Nothing is going on. I am not sleeping with Jack, no.

GRETA: Why does he come here?

MIMI: We're friends.

GRETA: He comes here, he makes you tapes. What the fuck is that? He makes you a chair.

MIMI: The chair is for me and my—my fiancé, God I hate that word, "fiancé."

GRETA: He comes here frequently. He never brings me.

MIMI: It's not that social.

GRETA: I don't get what that means.

MIMI: I assure you Greta ---

GRETA: You were together a long time.

MIMI: Before you were born.

GRETA: That's very patronizing.

MIMI: I'm sorry.

GRETA: Is it because I'm younger or because I'm an actress slash dancer that people frequently patronize me?

MIMI: I don't mean to patronize you.

GRETA: I'm aware of the humiliation of the slash. I'm aware that the thing that I do is a source of jokes told at my expense. That the way I express myself—through my body—what I like to do—is a joke to people.

(A pause; Mimi takes a cookie form the bag and eats it.)

GRETA: Jack believes in me and he makes me better. I'm a better person when I'm with him. And I know he loves me, and I love him better than anyone else can, and if you're still fucking him, what the hell is that?

MIMI: I'm engaged, for Christ's sake. I'm very happily with someone else.

GRETA: In that case, what are you doing hanging out with your ex-lover, letting him give you gifts, calling each other all the time—

MIMI: You know, Greta—let me tell you something—let me tell you something, Greta—

GRETA: Does your man appreciate that? Or is this some kind of weird— believe me, I've seen all kinds of weird perverted shit from middle-aged people who you'd never imagine—

(Slight pause.)

MIMI: I'm not middle-aged.

GRETA: Okay.

MIMI: When you get to be my age, one thing I can promise you that you will not feel is middle-aged.

(Greta says nothing.)

Jack is older than me, you know. He's quite a few years older. And anyway the point is that someday you will come to see that at a certain point in your life you come to value, to treasure, the people in your life and even when the relationship changes its nature you still want them in your life somehow. These people that have had this meaning in your life. These connections—you want to hold onto these rare and special connections in whatever form.

GRETA: That sounds like crap.

MIMI: And we don't call each other all the time. We're close. We speak. There's nothing wrong with that. You don't have any former boyfriends who you're still friends with?

GRETA: I could never just casually hang with someone I'd seen in the most intimate ways, stripped, raw, naked, fucking each other's brains out, humping and licking and sucking like beasts and knowing their secrets and their perversions and the way they smell, for him to know the way I smell, in the most intimate places, knowing every inch of each other and now we're just going to sit around and make polite chit -chat?

MIMI: Well everyone feels differently.

GRETA: I think that is fucking bizarre and hypocritical and only a person who can cut off part of themselves and live in denial, denial of intimacy, denial of the past—I could never do that.

MIMI: As I said, everyone's different.

GRETA: Your man doesn't mind?

MIMI: My "man" is not threatened, no.

GRETA: Do you buy that?

MIMI: He's stayed friends with a few ex-girlfriends and I don't mind. I don't mind at all, some of them I even like.

GRETA: He wants to fuck them.

MIMI: Listen Greta, you should go--

GRETA: Men always want that. Underneath. It's underneath everything.

MIMI: I think exes make wonderful friends – been there, done that, onward. I highly recommend it. In fact I wish I'd gone out with more people so I could have more former lovers now friends.

GRETA: In my opinion jealousy in a relationship is a sign of its strength, not its weakness.

MIMI: Okay. Greta. We could sit around debating this, but actually, I have to get to work. I've got what might be the only surviving letter from 12 years worth of intimate correspondence and that's really what I want to wrap my brain around right now, so you should talk to Jack about whatever it is you have to talk to him about. If things aren't working out in your relationship, it has absolutely nothing to do with me, I can promise you that.

GRETA: He told you that?

MIMI: What?

GRETA: That it isn't working out?

MIMI: You're here, aren't you?

GRETA: He visits you often, doesn't he.

MIMI: Greta ... break-ups are painful things. I'm not trying to be patronizing.

I went through some rough patches myself before Kai. Some really bad break-ups. And now I look back, and you know what? I'm grateful. Thank God. Thank God I got out. That's what you'll look back and think.

GRETA: I don't know why you keep insisting that we're breaking up. We've had some difficulties, okay, I'm sure he tells you that, I'm sure you know plenty of things about me that you shouldn't – same way I know things about you. Intimate things. But our sexual connection is better than ever, and to me that says a lot, that says the deepest thing.

MIMI: If you want my advice, Greta, which I'm quite sure that you don't, but since you came here, to my home, to my office, to my home office, I'm going to give it to you anyway—leave Jack. End it. Get on with your life.

GRETA: Why would you tell me that?

MIMI: Jack is a great guy, he's a wonderful friend, but he's a terrible boyfriend.

GRETA: You don't know what he's like now.

MIMI: Yes, I do.

GRETA: You don't know what he's like in a relationship. Unless you've been lying to me.

MIMI: I know—I know he's never going to be faithful to you. Okay? I'm sorry. He's not.

GRETA: Just because he wasn't faithful to you doesn't make him a faithless person.

(Greta stands to go.)

I'm going to tell him I was here myself.

MIMI: That's up to you.

GRETA: I was thinking I wouldn't, but I'm an honest person. I'd ask you not to mention it, but I doubt you'd keep your word on that.

(A pause.)

MIMI: Goodbye, Greta.

GRETA: Sorry about finishing your orange juice.

MIMI: Not at all.

(Mimi holds open the door as Greta exits.)

Elemeno Pea

Molly Smith Metzler

Comic
Devon, 35
Simone, 29

When Devon visits Simone for an end-of-summer sibs fest on Martha's Vineyard, she finds her little sister changed beyond recognition. As personal assistant to wealthy and demanding trophy wife Michaela Kell, Simone enjoys a lavish beachfront lifestyle that these girls never could have imagined growing up in blue-collar Buffalo; but is all this luxury really free of cost? Worlds collide and sisters square off in this keenly-observed comedy about ambition, regret and the choices that shape who we become.

SIMONE: Oh my god. She did way too much! Look at all this!

DEVON: Simone-- what the hell was that? That guy hates your ass.

SIMONE: Who? Him? He just has an attitude. (re: gift basket) Look! She got you a Black Dog sweatshirt! Aw! You have to try it on!

DEVON: Is it a problem that we're here?

SIMONE: Please? Please try it on? Then I can take a picture of you with my berry and text it to her as like a thank you, you love it so much kind of thing!

DEVON: *(putting on dumb sweatshirt)*
Simone, are we not supposed/to be here?

SIMONE: *(holding it up against her)*
AW! That looks so cute on you! Now smile and give me like a thumbs up and-- *(directing)*
You know what? No. I'm gonna do a short video instead. Say, "THANKS MICHAELA!" and wave.

DEVON: Absolutely not.

SIMONE: Say THANKS MICHAELA! YOUR HOME IS LOVELY! THANKS FOR HAVING ME AND FOR MY FERRY TICKET!

DEVON: Wait, what?
(not okay)
She bought my ferry ticket?

SIMONE: Oh, no, it's not like that. She has endless ferry passes and frequent flier miles.

DEVON: Simone! She paid for my flight too? You said you had miles.

SIMONE: Yeah but she has like two hundred billion thousand miles, ok, I'm filming! "Thanks Michaela for...." Go 'head Devon, hit it!

DEVON: *(to Simone's phone)*

"Well gee hi and thanks Michaela for paying for all of my transportation this weekend, which is not humiliating at all. Also, I'd like to send you a special thanks for the ginormous black dog sweatshirt. A black lab actually bit me in the face in 5th grade, so I can't tell you how excited I am to be wearing his doppleganger here on my chest. PS. Get a job!!!

SIMONE: Tay!!! I'll just send it without sound. That'll make her day. She's been a little sad this week-- I think it always makes her depressed when the season ends. Labor Day itself, you know? Time passing. Kids going back to school. Another year on the calendar. I think it can be a melancholy time of year-- sands through the hourglass.

DEVON: Simone. What the are you even talking about?

(Beat.)

SIMONE: You know, Devon. You should try to have more perspective about people.

DEVON: Should I.

SIMONE: The biggest thing I've learned this year with this job is that Mom and Mark raised us kind of narrow-mindedly. I mean, we know how to be hard workers, how to be totally self-sufficient, how to change a tire, but I don't think they did such an awesome job giving us perspective-- giving us empathy.

DEVON: And what is it that this lady's got you being so empathetic about, huh?

SIMONE: Never mind, I didn't mean to get into this.

DEVON: Yes you did.

SIMONE: No, I didn't.

DEVON: Her husband's a douche? Is that it?

SIMONE: No.

DEVON: How's he a douche?

SIMONE: He's not.

DEVON: What's he do that's douche-y?

SIMONE: I said never mind.

DEVON: How's/he a douche?

SIMONE: Devon! Seriously! I can't talk about this with you, ok? I signed a confidentiality agreement when I took this job.

DEVON: I showed you how to use a tampon, Simone. I showed you.

(Beat.)

SIMONE: Okay. Just. I don't know, yes. He can be a little....meticulous.

DEVON: How so?

SIMONE: I don't know... like this morning. When they were leaving for the airport, Michaela was in the kitchen and had her compact out to pluck a super-quick eyebrow hair with a tweezer. One quick hair, you know how you do, real quick, when you don't think anyone's looking?

DEVON: Yeah.

SIMONE: And, he just made a comment. He said something like, "don't forget the one on your chin."

(Beat.)

And... I think there's been other stuff like that. Like on a much larger scale.

(Beat.)

DEVON: What does she say when he says stuff like that?

SIMONE: I don't know. Nothing. Or like, she'll say thank you. Like it was nice of him to bring a chin pube to her attention. That's the thing about her, she just gives and gives. She's been so good to me this year.

DEVON: Yeah, you keep saying that; that she's so good to you. What does that mean, exactly?

SIMONE: I don't know, she's generous? And nice? We're sorta friends.

DEVON: You're sorta her employee, Simone.

SIMONE: See? This is why I don't tell you things, Devon. God! Because you become an interrogating freak and you get "crazy eyes" and everything's suspicious.

DEVON: I think it is suspicious that Jose calls her the wicked witch and you can't seem to give me one real, non-vague/example of how she's--

SIMONE: *(listing)*

She taught me how to play tennis.

She read my five hundred and ninety page novel.

She's been really cool about me dating Ethan. How are those?

DEVON: Why wouldn't she be cool with you dating whoever you want to date?

SIMONE: I don't know-- he's her husband's friend. It could be weird if she were less awesome. She also read my five hundred and ninety page novel, Devon, in case you didn't hear me say that just now.

DEVON: I read your novel, Simone, I just haven't had a chance to tell you that I did.

SIMONE: Yeah? What's the title?

DEVON: Well, whatever. What does your new BFF pay you, huh? Cuz that's the true test of friendship.

SIMONE: That's a very impolite quest--

DEVON: Look at you, all "that's a very impolite question." Girl, you're from
    Buffalo. I've seen you tailgating with a Boons fruit punch, rocking your
    puffy Bills starter jacket--

SIMONE: She pays me generously, okay?

DEVON: I want a figure. 20? 25? 30?...35? You can't make/more than 35--

SIMONE: Devon, there's a hostel in Oak Bluffs and I'll do it. I'll drop you
    there.

DEVON: Do it, bitch. I love hostels. 40? 45? Not 50. You do not make
    50fucking-k to babysit a rich lady with no kids and no job.
    (Beat.)
    Are you kidding me?! 51? 52? 53--

SIMONE: I make one hundred and four thousand dollars a year plus benefits,
    clothing allowance, room, board, and she paid off my student loans.
    (Beat.)

DEVON: *(genuinely alarmed)*
    Simone, what? Why in God's name would anyone pay off your student
    loans? I'm gonna be paying off my MSW until 2065.

SIMONE: Maybe that's what I'm worth.

DEVON: That's your "worth"? According to who?

SIMONE: I'll tell you whom: my placement service. Ivy league degree. Bilingual.
    I know html, outlook, and quick book. I type 85 words a minute with
    90% accuracy. I'm attractive. I'm able to--

DEVON: You're attractive?! Did you just say that?

SIMONE: So? It's a fact that when you're paid to be someone's public
    representative-- like an executive assistant-- being attractive ups your base
    salary.

DEVON: Like being a filthy prostitute?

SIMONE: Ok, I'm done. This is done. I knew I shouldn't have/invited you out
    here--

DEVON: You're twenty-seven, Simone! You're supposed to be hitch-hiking and
    seeing the world and having fun and sleeping with people named Skip,
    not making "monies" because you're attractive.

SIMONE: I'm twenty-nine, Devon.

DEVON: Well, whatever. Just! What do you do for that kind of money? Huh?

SIMONE: I'm the live-in executive assistant, Devon. I live-in and I executive-
    assist.

DEVON: Why can't you take a day off? All year you were like, this summer
    we're doing a sisters camping trip in the Berkshires! And all year you put
    me off/until finally I came to you--

SIMONE: Yes because I don't have any vacation days left, Devon! Because I used my entire allotment of vacation time to move you from New York to San Francisco, only to turn around three months later and fly out there to move you back!

DEVON: For which I've said thank you about three hundred times. But it's not like you gave me a kidney, Simone, you helped me move! Big whoop! I moved you to Boston!

SIMONE: You helped me move a bed to Boston, Devon. And you abandoned me halfway up the stairs because/you had Celtics tickets--

DEVON: That is revisionist history! Revisionist hist--

SIMONE: Look, I have empathy and perspective about everything you've been through, ok? I'm sorry that you screwed the pooch with California. I'm sorry that you quit your entire life for some dude you didn't know. But that doesn't mean you get to show up here with your crazy eyes and poop all over my great gig, especially when I have been so there for you this year.

DEVON: There for me?! I'm back at Mom's house! I'm basically in a van down by the river here and I haven't seen you in six months! Don't you give a shit about what's going on with me?!

SIMONE: Of course I do, Devon! Of course I do! That's why i invited you out here FOR A REALLY FUN BDAY WEEKEND!

DEVON: WELL MY FUCKING BDAY WAS THREE MONTHS AGO AND YOU DIDN'T BOTHER TO SHOW! AND YOU LOOK LIKE A RETARDED EASTER EGG IN THAT GETUP!

SIMONE: WELL EXCUSE ME FOR WANTING TO SHARE MY BEACHFRONT SUCCESS WITH YOUR BASEMENT-DWELLING FRAGGLE ROCK ASS—

DEVON:	SIMONE:
I CANNOT *BELIEVE* YOU LET SOME DUMB BITCH GET Her BLACK AMEX OUT AND PAY FOR ME TO COME TO HERE! I WOULD RATHER INHERIT AUNT TERRY'S GLANDS THAN DO THAT TO YOU, YOU MONKEY'S BUTT WHORE FACE J.CREW WANNA BE SELL OUT—	YOU IMMATURE, UNGRACIOUS PERSON! GOD! YOU ARE JEALOUS OF EVERYTHING I DO! IT'S DISGUSTING! TO THINK I WAS *ACTUALLY* LOOKING FORWARD TO YOU COMING! I WANTED TO IMPRESS YOUR JUDGMENTAL, ALMOST-FORTY YEAR-OLD ASS!--

Goodbye New York, Goodbye Heart

Lally Katz

Seriocomic
CAROLine, late 20s
Miss Jacklyn, mid-30s

> *In this scene, which takes place in MySpace New York, where everyone is either a suicide or an avalanche dweller, Miss Jacklyn compares herself to Caroline, letting Caroline know that she was once just like her, which indicates that Caroline will end up just like Miss Jacklyn. However, Caroline doesn't see this as a bad thing, as she wants to stay in Myspace New York and live with a suicide, and it seems that Miss Jacklyn has found a permanent way to do that.*

MISS JACKLYN: You haven't been here long.

CAROLINE: No. Tonight is my trial.

MISS JACKLYN: I mean in Myspace New York. You haven't been here long.

CAROLINE: No.

MISS JACKLYN: I like your look. I used to look like you. Before I died my hair.

CAROLINE: You used to have the same hair colour as me?

MISS JACKLYN: Practically.

CAROLINE: It looks good that colour. The one you have now.

MISS JACKLYN: Only with make-up. You can't have this many highlights and then go natural on your face. I'm always dressing up to match my hair these days.

CAROLINE: I like your leopard print.

MISS JACKLYN: Do I look like I'm trying to be sexy?

CAROLINE: You do look sexy.

MISS JACKLYN: That's sweet of you to say. But do I look like I'm trying?

CAROLINE: Well isn't it good to try and look nice?

MISS JACKLYN: I don't look effortless, do I?

(Caroline gives an awkward smile and shrug.)

MISS JACKLYN: I will probably never look effortless again in my life. Neither will you after a while Caroline

CAROLINE: Well that's okay, because things are different here. Everyone's glamorous. I mean look, all you ladies have had your nails done and your toenails done. Things are just raised a notch higher here. I like it. I'll spray my hair with leave-in shine tomorrow.

MISS JACKLYN: That's nice. To care about the little things. I'm the same. I care about it for Tom. My Tommy.

CAROLINE: Is he your boyfriend?

MISS JACKLYN: No. He was my high school sweetheart. Would you believe I've been married twice- both times to men that weren't him? But it was always him I loved- I'd pretend in my head it wasn't- but my heart was never fooled. Then after his suicide, I just packed up my life back there- that's a lie. I slept around first. I tried to find another him in every bar in Delaware. That's my birthplace. But again, my heart knew. So here I am. The President of Avalanche Dweller's Anonymous. In Myspace New York.

CAROLINE: Are you scared for when it crashes?

MISS JACKLYN: No. Because I've made a home here. For me and Tommy.

CAROLINE: A home? Where?

MISS JACKLYN: In a really good neighbourhood. In a safe neighbourhood.

CAROLINE: So he lives there with you? Tom- Tommy?

MISS JACKLYN: He will. He hasn't moved in yet. He's very busy. You know how it is. All the suicides have so many causes. But soon he'll come in with his boxes. He has no idea how much furniture I've gotten!

CAROLINE: So if I got an apartment- I could stay here? With a suicide?

MISS JACKLYN: It's more than that. To make a permanent home, you have to give your life to it.

CAROLINE: I'll do that. I'll give him my life.

MISS JACKLYN: I can help you. I know someone in real estate.

CAROLINE: That would be wonderful.

MISS JACKLYN: Who is it? Who's the suicide?

CAROLINE: Thornbury. I know him. And he knows me.

(Miss Jacklyn looks at her. After a while, she nods.)

MISS JACKLYN: There's no length too far, to go for someone you love. Make them a home, somewhere you can really comfort them in. Oh this lonely window, from my hallway to the world.

CAROLINE: I'll make him a home. I'll bake him lasagne. I'll give him my life.

MISS JACKLYN: And then.

CAROLINE: Lasagne every night.

(Miss Jacklyn smiles at Caroline)

MISS JACKLYN: You look just like me. When I first got here. Pretty much exactly the same colour hair. It's so nice. But you could get maybe get a couple of highlights towards the front. Just to brighten it up around your face. For Thornbury. To cheer him up.

Goodbye New York, Goodbye Heart

Lally Katz

Seriocomic
CAROLINE, late 20s
Kim Ann, mid-20s

We are in MySpace New York, where everyone is either a suicide or an avalanche dweller. Caroline is new in Myspace New York, and Kim Ann is a suicide there. Kim Ann is very popular with the male suicides, but is strongly disliked by the female Avalanche Dwellers. In this scene, Kim Ann has approached Caroline, apparently trying to make friends. However, Caroline is suspicious and possibly feels threatened by Kim Ann. Kim Ann senses this and becomes emotional and hurt. Their conversation ends dramatically and awkwardly.

CAROLINE is cleaning up. Kim Ann approaches her. Kim Ann I'm Kim Ann Is there any food left?

CAROLINE: Yeah, I think there's plenty.

KIM ANN: Do you mind if I take a plate of it home with me? I like to have something to give the little girl next door.

CAROLINE: I'm sure that's fine.

(Caroline gets a plate of food ready for her.)

KIM ANN: I hear you're from a town in Australia.

CAROLINE: That's right. I hear you were born in Honolulu.

KIM ANN: Yeah. I was. These canapés look great. I would try them, but I don't really eat.

CAROLINE: No, you don't look like you eat. You look like you're too thin to eat.

KIM ANN: A lot of women hate me for that. But seriously, this is the honest to God truth- since I've been a suicide- I really haven't had an appetite.

CAROLINE: I believe you. Besides I don't mind that you're thin. I don't think it means you have an eating disorder. A lot of the time, people are just jealous when they say a thin person has an eating disorder.

KIM ANN: I did have one. Back when I was alive, I had an eating disorder. Caroline It's bold of you to say it.

KIM ANN: Nothing bold about honesty. Hey, you know the music system they've got on their computer here?

CAROLINE: No.

KIM ANN: Well it's the new I-tunes. You can download free emotions on it. You can get nine free emotions in an hour. Do you know their password?

CAROLINE: No. This is only my first shift. And it's a trial shift.

KIM ANN: Oh, well you should find out and we can download some sometime. Watch this.

(Kim Ann begins to cry. And she stops immediately and laughs.)

KIM ANN: I had two before I got here. They've almost worn off now. They've left me kind of soft. Everyone's soft when you catch them on their own though I guess, after they've been run through with emotion. You can download almost anything here. That's why I like it. I never have to say who I am two days in a row. Or if I do and change my mind no one's allowed to hold it against me. I'm allowed to be fascinating. Cool huh?

CAROLINE: Yeah. That's cool.

KIM ANN: I mean I've gone through some shit in my time. But not anymore. No pain. Not anymore. Only joy and love and nurturing. That's where I'm at now.

CAROLINE: I'm really glad for you. Kim Ann You don't seem like it. Caroline What do you mean?

KIM ANN: You don't seem like you're glad for me. You seem like you don't like me.

CAROLINE: I've been very polite to you.

KIM ANN: Exactly. Which is how I can tell you don't like me. I've given you three openings now to start a girly chitchat and you haven't taken one.

CAROLINE: When did you?

KIM ANN: First I said you're from Australia. Next I told you I'd had an eating disorder. Third I said we should download emotions together. And you didn't fly with any of those openings.

CAROLINE: I'm sorry I missed them. It's so late and I've been working.

KIM ANN: You don't like me. You're going to end up just like those other women. You are. Because you're not going to try and be anything else.

CAROLINE: What do you think I should try and be?

KIM ANN: Maybe just don't try putting a cover on every book you see. You don't know what it was like to live and die as me.

(Kim Ann takes the plate of food and leaves.)

The Housewives of Mannheim

Alan Brody

Dramatic
Billie, 29
May, 29

> *May and Billie have just returned from a party where both of them have had*
> *a little too much to drink. May has found a new friend in Sophie Birnbaum,*
> *an older woman who is a refugee from the Nazis in Europe. It is 1944.*

MAY: *(Off)*
Come on in. The house feels funny when it's empty like this, and so late.

BILLIE: *(Off)*
It's only two o'clock.

MAY: *(Coming into the kitchen with Billie. May is wearing the outfit Billie*
brought to show her in the previous scene.)
I haven't been out this late since my sister Sarah's affair. And then I was
with Lenny. It feels funny to be up so late alone. We should go upstairs
and check on the kids.

BILLIE: They're asleep. If anything was wrong Rhett Butler would have called.
Let's have another drink.

MAY: All I've got is some schnapps. For when Lenny's father comes over.

BILLIE: That's fine.

MAY: That's the men's drink.

BILLIE: May. . .

MAY: You make it. I never know how much.
(Looking out the window)
The street's so quiet. There's one car stopped at the light. Makes you feel
like you want to stay up every night just to see it like that.
(Going back to the light switch)
You mind if I turn this out? It seems so harsh this late.
(She turns out the light. The room is lit only by the oblique light from the hall)
Everything looks so different now. In the dark, so late at night. When I
was a kid I used to think all the furniture in the house would disappear
when everyone was asleep. And it would come back as soon as my mother
opened her eyes. I always wanted to stay up to see what all the rooms
looked like with nothing in them. Now I see. It doesn't disappear. It just.
. .shimmers.

BILLIE: Shimmers?

MAY: Look at my old table. It looks like if I touch it my hand will go right through. You, too. The way the light's touching your hair and your shoulders.

BILLIE: How did you like the party?

MAY: Everybody was laughing a lot. I didn't understand what was funny.

BILLIE: You were sitting in the corner so quiet.

MAY: That man, Bob, was nice. He talked to me for a long time. He's a schoolteacher. Third grade. That's very unusual. I couldn't figure out who he came with.

BILLIE: Why didn't you ask him?

MAY: I didn't want him to think. . .

BILLIE: What.

MAY: I was interested.

BILLIE: Were you?

MAY: I can't be like you.

BILLIE: What's like me?

MAY: I don't know.

BILLIE: A lot of people asked me about you.

MAY: Who?

BILLIE: Now it's okay to be interested.

MAY: I want to know if it's someone I talked to, or just someone who looked at me.

BILLIE: Gloria Scanlon. The one with the brown and orange scarf. And Beverly Cohen. The bobbed red hair.

MAY: Women.

BILLIE: Women aren't allowed to be interested?

MAY: I just thought you meant interested interested. I didn't think you meant interested.

BILLIE: What if I meant interested interested?

MAY: I can see Sophie's kitchen window from here. Sometimes the light's still on when I'm getting ready for bed. She stays up very late.

BILLIE: Which one is it?

MAY: Over and up. 4-D.

BILLIE: It's dark now.

MAY: It's dark everywhere. Except for Baumgarten up on your floor.

BILLIE: She leaves it on all the time.

MAY: It feels funny to have my light on this late. The electric company is going to call and ask me why I'm up so late.

BILLIE: If they do, I'll tell them. I'll say you're in love.

MAY: It really is late. Maybe we better- - -

BILLIE: I was in love like that. Twelve years old.

MAY: I'm twenty-nine.

BILLIE: Miss Nagelson, taught dramatics at the Settlement House on the weekends. Short, black hair cut just like a man's, with a part and everything, smoked Chesterfields, would light each one with the one she just finished, and always wore suits with shoulder bags. Once I followed her home on the subway all the way to the Bronx to find out where she lived. After that I would sneak out of school to go by her house and just look up at her window. Just like you're looking up at Sophie Birnbaum's.

MAY: Women don't fall in love with other women.

BILLIE: You never heard of it.

MAY: Not in Brooklyn.

BILLIE: You're up there all the time.

MAY: She lets me listen to her practice. Even with the arthritis. . .She says she was even better when she was young. She's going to bring me some records she made. I can hear what she sounded like then.

BILLIE: You barely have time for anyone else.

MAY: She tells me about what's happening in Europe.

BILLIE: It's O.K. to be in love with her.

MAY: It's not.

BILLIE: Why not?

MAY: Because then it would be okay for anybody to be in love with anybody.

BILLIE: And that's not a good thing.

MAY: No.

BILLIE: Like me and Miss Nagelson.

MAY: You were a little girl. That's different.

BILLIE: From what?

MAY: From now.

BILLIE: From if you were in love with Sophie?

MAY: Yes.

BILLIE: Or I was in love with you.

(There is a hesitation while May decides how seriously to take it.)

What if I told you I look to see if the light in your window is on every night?

MAY: I wouldn't believe you.

BILLIE: Maybe everybody in the apartment house is looking to see if somebody else's light is on every night. All of us standing there in the dark, peeking out, afraid somebody might catch us at it. Or maybe hoping somebody will.

MAY: I never know when you're making a joke.

BILLIE: Yes, you do.

MAY: I got a letter from Lenny this morning. He says- - -
> *(Billie kisses May on the lips)*
I don't know what to do with that.

BILLIE: What do you want to do?

MAY: I don't know.

BILLIE: You're shaking.

MAY: I don't know why.
> *(Billie kisses her again)*
You're my friend.

BILLIE: I've wanted to do that for ten years. You knew that, didn't you?

MAY: Yes.

BILLIE: Then let me- - -

MAY: You're scaring me.

BILLIE: You're learning new things. You don't have to be afraid of anything new anymore.

MAY: It's wrong.

BILLIE: You're beautiful, May.

MAY: Don't say that. Not that way. Like the men say it.

BILLIE: I'm a woman. I won't make you feel like the men do. Let me-

MAY: No. It would spoil everything.

BILLIE: It doesn't have to.

MAY: Everything is happening so fast.

BILLIE: You're changing.
> *(Billie slowly, carefully, begins stroking May's hair, gradually working down to her shoulders)*

MAY: Yes.

BILLIE: You want it all.

MAY: I can't change that much.

BILLIE: Your breasts.

MAY: Yes.

BILLIE: I know how to touch them.

MAY: Do you really want me?

BILLIE: Yes.

MAY: Everything will change.

BILLIE: Nothing.

MAY: Everything.

In the Wake

Lisa Kron

Dramatic
Ellen, mid-30s
Amy, mid-30s

> *While she is attending a conference at a university Ellen, a political activist, meets Amy, an experimental film maker whose interest in Ellen does not have to do with her political views.*

> *(Ellen and Amy in a chair somewhere outside a lecture hall somewhere on the Harvard campus. The event is long over and they're the only ones left. Amy watches Ellen raptly while she talks.)*

AMY: *(trying to figure it out)*
..But... but... Wait. I'm lost. I thought you said you were writing about strip malls.

ELLEN: No, no, I'm writing about the tax code -

AMY: Okay?

ELLEN: --My example is strip malls.

AMY: *(beat as Amy contemplates, then decides she needs further explanation)*
More.

ELLEN: Okay.

AMY: Okay.

ELLEN: Stick with me -

AMY: I will.

ELLEN: 'cause this is good.

AMY: I believe you.

ELLEN: Alright, the thing people don't realize about strip malls is that the reason they're everywhere, is that in the 1950's Congress made a tiny change to the tax code accelerating the depreciation rate for new construction -

AMY: Okay...?

ELLEN: And the reason they put it there was to encourage manufacturing but what it actually did -- was create a tax loophole that made it profitable for developers to build strip malls in non-populated areas. And that's why strip malls are everywhere. These boring, little infrastructures matter.

AMY: Aha.

ELLEN: But we don't see it because Americans are dedicated to the myth that we're all operating independently and I'm not just talking about motherfucking libertarians who think all humans act in a self interested vacuum, Alan Greenspan and his Ayn Rand bullshit, fucking libertarians drive me crazy, no, no, no, I'm talking about us on the left. Somehow we are incapable of thinking systemically or politically. Our whole strategy seems to be to find some magic personality to make it 1968 again , while - okay, okay, okay, this is the thing: somebody is thinking systemically and it's Karl Rove and the Club for Growth guys. While we're putting all of our energy into praying for another Kennedy, they are making a million tiny changes to the tax code, to media regulation, to anti-trust protections, to election laws and they are successfully channeling money, power and votes their way and we can't figure out what is going on. We're like "Waaaait a minute. Waaait a minute. What's going on?"

These systems matter because... because... Because, look - when the American Revolution was over, the logical thing for the framers to do would have been to say: "Okay. King George out. Our guy is in. Thank you very much. Now go back to your candle dipping." But they had this vision of a dynamic society and they believed the only way to create that was systemically. All those brilliant men and they didn't just put one of them in charge. Instead they created this system, this carefully constructed series of conduits through which people's energies and aspirations could flow, It's the thing that just... moves me about this country. It's the thing that just... just slays me about this country -- that it was set up to be a place where people could change -- that the whole idea was to allow people to change their status, change their lives - was that your question? I'm sorry, I got off track, what was your question again?

AMY: You have a beautiful mouth.

ELLEN: What?

AMY: You have a beautiful mouth. People must tell you that.

ELLEN: What? Uh. No. Not so much.

AMY: I really like watching you talk.

ELLEN: *(flustered)*

Good thing. I talk a lot.

AMY: I'm sorry. Go on.

ELLEN: Well I lost my train of thought.

AMY: The framers?

ELLEN: The framers... the framers... I don't know. I can't remember what I was saying. *(Looks around, startled)*

Weren't there a lot of people here? Where did everybody go?

AMY: I don't know.

ELLEN: My ass hurts!

AMY: I think we've been sitting here a while.

ELLEN: What time is it? Didn't the panel just end? It's dark out.

AMY: *(looks at her watch)*

It's nine. We've been here four hours.

ELLEN: Really? Oh my god. Wow. I talk a lot! I'm sure you wanna get home. Or to your studio. Do you work late? You probably want to get back to your clay.

AMY: Clay?

ELLEN: I don't know why I assumed clay. What kind of sculpture do you do?

AMY: *(amused)*

I'm a film-maker.

ELLEN: How did I get sculptor?

AMY: I have no idea.

ELLEN: Sculptor. Hmm. Do you sculpt anything?

AMY: No.

ELLEN: Did you tell me you were a film maker?

AMY: Yeah.

ELLEN: I'm sorry.

AMY: It's okay. I called you out of the blue when I saw you were coming to Harvard.

ELLEN: I'm so embarrassed. Okay so films. About what? Did you tell me that already, too?

AMY: No. Uh... Well, I'm kind of starting a new thing - but the films I'm known for -- you know, to the extent that I'm known -- are collections of fleeting images of everyday things - They're short - a minute each. Short and Intense. My signature style. Sadly.

ELLEN: What are they about?

AMY: They're... Ah. If I could give you a clear articulation I'd get so many more grants. I actually want people not to think about them too much. I want them to be ... felt.

ELLEN: Huh.

(Beat.)

AMY: Were you surprised when I called you?

ELLEN: I don't know. Yeah. . I don't know.

AMY: You remembered me.

ELLEN: Well... yeah, I mean.. Whenever you were home from college your sister gave us daily reports. It was a big event in the debate team. She was so dazzled by you.

AMY: Yeah, well...

ELLEN: I'm surprised you remember me.

AMY: I remember you because you seemed so... brave.

ELLEN: Brave? Me? I was afraid of everything all the time.

AMY: Really?

ELLEN: I had to teach myself to be brave.

AMY: How do you do that?

ELLEN: I don't know... at some point I thought - if I get to the end of my life and realize I didn't do all these things because I was afraid I'm going to be so pissed. I couldn't bear that.

(Beat.)

AMY: You think a lot.

ELLEN: I do.

AMY: I feel a lot. Too much, really.

ELLEN: How can you feel too much? I can't imagine it.

(Amy shrugs.)

AMY: My sister showed me that article about you in the Times.

ELLEN: Wow. She must read the Times really carefully.

AMY: Well, she was very impressed.

ELLEN: How's she doing?

AMY: She's good. She's married. Three kids. My dad lives down the street from them - he moved there when my mom passed away a few of years ago. They're all family, family... And... I think I'm not really cut out for that kind of family life.

ELLEN: Not everybody wants the same kind of life.

AMY: Yeah. No, I want it. I want it a lot, actually. But maybe not, you know. Maybe not really, or I'd have it, right?

ELLEN: I don't know about that. Maybe you just don't have it yet.

AMY: Maybe it doesn't want me.

ELLEN: It's okay, we don't have to talk about it.

ELLEN: We can talk about it.

AMY: I don't want to.

ELLEN: So... you said you're doing something new with your films?

AMY: I did?

ELLEN: I thought // you did -

AMY: Oh yeah. Yeah. Uh... Well... I've been thinking about negative space... or, I mean, my relationship to negative space.

ELLEN: Negative space...?

AMY: It's... Have you ever taken a drawing class?

ELLEN: No.

AMY: Me neither, actually. But I was teaching myself to draw -

ELLEN: You were? That's so industrious.

AMY: Is it?

ELLEN: I'm sorry. Go on.

AMY: -well, there's a basic exercise you do when you're learning to draw where you draw the negative space.

ELLEN: Which means...?

AMY: It means you don't focus on the object you're drawing, you draw the space around it. So if I was drawing your hand -

(taking Ellen's hand in hers)

I wouldn't draw your fingers. Instead I'd look at the shapes of these spaces between your fingers - this is negative space. Your hand is positive space. And when you draw with this exercise the drawings are... almost unsettling, they're so vivid. You really see the thing. You really see the hand. Somehow by focusing on what it's not you end up with an intense... an intense sense of what it is.

ELLEN: *(flustered, taking her hand back)*

Oh, uh-huh

AMY: Negative space is also an idea in architecture. It's open space. Space that's... undefined. It makes people uncomfortable. They instinctively more toward positive spaces where the boundaries are clear. It's not unrelated to what you were saying before about Jane Jacobs.

ELLEN: Oh, Jane Jacobs. I do love her so.

AMY: Well, of course. She's all about infrastructure and flow. I always want to make the intelligent design people read her.

ELLEN: Why?

AMY: Because... Okay, their central argument is: "There must have been a plan." And Jane Jacobs says the opposite. She says that cities only work when they're not completely planned, when there's space for unplanned juxtapositions and unexpected encounters... for randomness.

ELLEN: Yes.

AMY: *(continuing)*

And... It's... It's such an important idea. Because any artist will tell you, any scientist will tell you, that it's the accident, it's the mistake, that causes you to re-frame and expand everything. Nothing really amazing is created by one mind thinking rationally. The intelligent design argument is absurd! They say there's no possible way something so complex and amazing as the universe could have been an accident and so it must have come from one rational mind. But nothing really extraordinary happens without some irrational

AMY: *(cont.)*

leap. We don't leave our comfort zone easily right? People who want to lead big lives and think big thoughts - they know a wrench in the works, well, it might not be pleasant but it will get them to the next place. They're willing to let themselves be knocked off track.

ELLEN: I agree but for some reason people are afraid of that.

AMY: Some of them. Yes. Well, of course they are.

ELLEN: Because... flux is very uncomfortable.

ELLEN: But I don't get it. You can think you're choosing certainty but you get strip malls and George Bush. How can that be more comfortable?

AMY: Lots of people grapple with complexity. But... complexity is scary.

ELLEN: To me it feels obvious.

AMY: The things that matter, the huge, magnificent things, the big three -- Art, Religion, Sex... each of them can take us to the highest place -- or the lowest. You know? Each of them offers transcendence -- and also degradation. I think probably that's what makes them... the biggest things.

ELLEN: You're very smart. You're a smarty-pants.

(Amy shrugs. A little embarrassed.) (Beat.)

AMY: Do you and Danny planning to have kids?

ELLEN: No. Kayla and Laurie are.

AMY: But not you?

ELLEN: Maybe. I don't know. I feel... I'm ambivalent. It's that thing of wanting to stay open to the injection of randomness.

AMY: I think having kids is probably one injection of randomness after another, actually.

ELLEN: Probably so. Yes, that makes sense. We talk about it sometimes. Maybe we will. Are you thinking you want to have kids?

AMY: I want so much.

(Beat.)

Wanna hear something funny?

ELLEN: When I saw that piece about you in the Times I thought: That's the person I'm going to marry. And then one second later I thought: Oh. No. She's already married.

ELLEN: That is funny.

AMY: I know.

And so I called you.

ELLEN: Well. Huh.

AMY: Yeah. It's funny.

(Beat.)

ELLEN: I'm not speechless that often.

AMY: It's okay. I know you're with Danny. I just wanted to see you. I'm glad that I called you.

ELLEN: I'm glad, too. I didn't really know you then - it's funny - as kids. But I feel now - I don't know - something... familiar...?

AMY: Yes.

(Beat.)

I feel kind of scared.

ELLEN: You do? Why?

AMY: I don't know. It's okay.

(Ellen grabs and playfully shakes her.)

ELLEN: You! What's going on here?

AMY: I don't know. Something.

(Ellen lets go of her.)

AMY: How many more days are you in Boston?

ELLEN: Four.

AMY: Huh.

ELLEN: What?

(Amy gives her a look.)

ELLEN: I know. I have to get the hell out of town!

(Amy takes Ellen's head in her hands. She captures Ellen's gaze and holds it as she leans in with slow, deliberate intensity, to kiss her - her lips are slightly parted. Ellen's as well, their lips just brushing in electric intensity. Their eyes close, their breath flows and catches as they are lost in this kiss. Then they come apart.)

AMY: I shouldn't have done that.

ELLEN: No. It's okay.

AMY: I'm a little slain by you.

ELLEN: I'm... I'm...

AMY: I feel a little overwhelmed. I feel a little scared.

ELLEN: Oh no. It's okay. This - um. You know. Nothing is happening. I mean -- . This is... this is probably the best part anyway. Right? I mean... this part is probably better than sex.

AMY: *(with complete unguarded sincerity)*

Oh no. I'm sure sex would be much better.

Jailbait

Deirdre O'Connor

Seriocomic
Claire, 15
Emmy, 15

Emmy and Claire, high school sophomores, get ready for an evening at a club where they will try to pass as college students and hook up with older men.

(Lights up on a teenage girl's bedroom. The room still shows the now embarrassing signs of childhood. There are unicorn sheets on the bed and several stuffed animals strewn about.

It is early in the evening and the last traces of daylight stream through the window where Emmy, fifteen, stands staring outside. Her clothes are expensive and fashionable and she appears out of place in what looks like a child's bedroom. Claire, also fifteen, enters carrying a bottle of white wine. Claire lacks Emmy's style. She notices a stuffed animal on display and quickly drops it on the floor and kicks it under the bed. Claire pulls the cork out of the wine and sniffs the bottle.)

CLAIRE: Does wine go bad?

EMMY: I don't know, does it smell bad?

CLAIRE: Kind of, yeah.

(Claire takes a sip. It tastes like vinegar.)

You want some?

EMMY: She's not gone yet.

CLAIRE: Really?

EMMY: She's still like right outside.

(Emmy takes the bottle from Claire.)

If that bothers you.

CLAIRE: *(Bluffing)*

It doesn't bother me.

(Pause)

I mean- She's not... Looking in at us or...

EMMY: No.

CLAIRE: So, it doesn't bother me.

EMMY: OK.

(Emmy takes a sip from the bottle.)

This tastes like refrigerator.

CLAIRE: I know.

> *(Emmy plugs her nose and takes another sip.)*

At least we know my Mom won't miss it.

> *(Emmy looks out the window.)*

EMMY: It's a cute top she's got on.

CLAIRE: It's mine.

EMMY: Really? It looks good on her.

CLAIRE: I didn't really notice.

EMMY: So, who's the guy? With your Mom?

CLAIRE: That's Charlie.

EMMY: Oh.

CLAIRE: He's just a friend.

EMMY: He opened her door.

CLAIRE: So?

EMMY: So he opened her car door. I'm just saying.

CLAIRE: That's just manners.

EMMY: Oh.

CLAIRE: They're just friends.

EMMY: OK.

> *(Emmy continues to watch the couple through the window. Claire moves over to the window and looks out.)*

CLAIRE: He's my Dad's friend, really.

EMMY: Oh.

CLAIRE: His friend from work. I think she's just being nice.

> *(Claire moves back to the bureau.)*

EMMY: Yeah. And she's laughing so... At least she's not having a bad time.

CLAIRE: She's laughing?

EMMY: Yeah. She looks young. I don't think of your Mom as young. And there they go.

> *(Claire is silent.)*

Looks like we're in the clear.

CLAIRE: Good. That's good.

> *(Pause.)*

Will you do my make-up?

EMMY: Why?

CLAIRE: I don't know. I want to look different. If I do it, I'll just look like me. Like always.

EMMY: OK.

> *(Emmy rifles through the make-up on the dresser. She selects a bottle.)*

Chanel?

CLAIRE: It's my mom's. She just - she splurged or something.

EMMY: Wow. Some of it hasn't even been opened yet. Will she be pissed if we use it?

CLAIRE: Whatever. Just use what you want.

EMMY: OK.

(Emmy begins to apply Claire's make-up.)

CLAIRE: Were you nervous? I mean, last time.

EMMY: I was nervous. Sure.

CLAIRE: Because it's illegal?

EMMY: We're fifteen. Everything fun is illegal.

(Emmy takes another sip of wine to illustrate her point.)

CLAIRE: Right.

EMMY: Besides, it's barely illegal. I mean, it's call-your-parents illegal, not send-you-to-juvie illegal.

CLAIRE: Yeah. I'm not nervous.

EMMY: Good.

(Emmy passes the bottle to Claire.)

I'm glad you're coming.

CLAIRE: Yeah?

EMMY: I didn't think you'd be cool with this.

CLAIRE: Why not?

EMMY: I don't know. You haven't... been around much lately.

CLAIRE: I've been around.

EMMY: At school. Not after. It's like you're always with your Mom or something.

CLAIRE: Well, tonight I'm with you.

EMMY: Yeah, you are!

(Emmy continues with the make-up.)

CLAIRE: You think I'll pass?

EMMY: Absolutely.

(Pause.)

You do have a padded bra right?

CLAIRE: No.

EMMY: *(disappointed)*

Oh.

CLAIRE: Am I supposed to?

EMMY: Well... it's probably OK. I wouldn't worry about it.

CLAIRE: OK.

(Pause)

EMMY: Just, maybe...

CLAIRE: What?

EMMY: Maybe you should stand behind me. At the door. In case it's a problem.

CLAIRE: You really think it's a problem?

EMMY: No. I'm sure it's not. We'll focus on your other features.

CLAIRE: But boobs are important?

EMMY: If you don't have ID.

CLAIRE: You're trying to make me nervous.

EMMY: No I'm not. I'm just... Strategizing.

CLAIRE: If we don't get in do we just not get in or is it like when you get caught shop-lifting and they drag you off to that little room?

EMMY: Claire, it's a club not Urban Outfitters.

CLAIRE: I know, but--

EMMY: Don't worry about it. Last week the guy hardly even looked at me.

CLAIRE: Last week you were with your older sister.

EMMY: And this time I'm with you. Relax. I highly doubt there's a "little room."

CLAIRE: Good.

EMMY: And even if there is, I mean what's the worst that could happen? They call our Dads and we get grounded or something? Big deal.
(Pause, realizing what she just said)
I mean... Well, not your Dad.

CLAIRE: *(brushing it off)*
No. Yeah. I get it.

EMMY: I'm sorry, that was stupid.

CLAIRE: No. It's fine.

EMMY: I just meant...

CLAIRE: Emmy. It's fine.
(Claire looks at herself in the mirror.)
I need mascara.

EMMY: Right. I'm not done yet.

CLAIRE: I want a dramatic look. Not every-day high school. Dramatic.

EMMY: I think I can handle it, Claire.
(Emmy continues to apply.)

CLAIRE: She doesn't usually go out.

EMMY: Who?

CLAIRE: My mom.

EMMY: Oh.

CLAIRE: She stays home a lot. Just lately...

EMMY: Charlie.

CLAIRE: Right. I just didn't want you to think she's... I don't know... Dating or...

EMMY: I don't think anything.

CLAIRE: Good. Because she's not. She's still not ready.

EMMY: OK.

CLAIRE: And anyway it's good. That I don't have to... You know. Stay home with her again. I can just go out. I can just have one night out. I mean, finally. Right?

EMMY: Right. Finally.

(Claire takes another sip from the wine.)

CLAIRE: What's it like inside?

EMMY: The club? I don't know. Dark. We'll stand by the bar. My sister says if you stand by the bar eventually everyone will see you. It's the most social.

CLAIRE: OK.

(Pause)

And that's where you met him?

EMMY: Yeah.

CLAIRE: And he was, I don't know, he was nice to you?

EMMY: Sure.

CLAIRE: I was just- I was just wondering.

EMMY: They're just over-twenty-one. They're not like girl-crazed date-rape machines.

CLAIRE: I know.

EMMY: They actually have less of all that high school boy constant-boner bullshit, so it's better really.

CLAIRE: Right. I mean, that's what I figured.

EMMY: Just breathe, Claire.

CLAIRE: I'm breathing.

EMMY: You're gonna meet someone.

CLAIRE: I know.

(Pause)

EMMY: Then you talk to him.

CLAIRE: Right. Right.

EMMY: Claire, you talk to boys all the time.

CLAIRE: I know. I'm just- Usually I'm not lying.

EMMY: Don't think of it as lying. Think of it as... Improv. But in a bar.

CLAIRE: Improv.

EMMY: Yeah.

CLAIRE: Can I use my own name?

EMMY: Of course. You use as many real details as possible so there's less chance of a slip-up.

CLAIRE: Right.

EMMY: And you have to be confident. No pulling at your clothes or anything. No slouching. No crossing your arms over your boobs. You have to act like you dress like that every day.

CLAIRE: What else?

EMMY: You have to perfect your back-story.

CLAIRE: Back-story?

EMMY: It's the age lie. You know, the little details that add up to twenty-one.

CLAIRE: Ok, what's yours?

(Emmy strikes her best Miss America pose.)

EMMY: I'm a junior at Sarah Lawrence and I hope someday to teach kindergarten.

CLAIRE: Kindergarten? You hate kids.

EMMY: Whatever. It creates a whole nurturing image. Men like a nurturing image.

CLAIRE: OK, what's my back-story then?

EMMY: You're a college student. At Harvard.

CLAIRE: Can we say Emerson or something? I'm not even sure if I'll get into Harvard.

EMMY: No you can not say Emerson I already told them you go to Harvard.

CLAIRE: What?

EMMY: Nothing. Let's pick your major.

CLAIRE: You told who I go to Harvard?

EMMY: I forget.

CLAIRE: Emmy.

EMMY: Just a guy.

CLAIRE: Are you pimping me out?

EMMY: No. A little. We're more like... Just meeting them.

CLAIRE: Just meeting who?

EMMY: The guy. My guy. From last week.

CLAIRE: Emmy!

EMMY: Well, he swears his friend is cute.

CLAIRE: This is a setup? When were you going to tell me that this is a setup?

EMMY: I wasn't. I thought we'd just get there and you'd figure it out. It's more fun that way.

CLAIRE: This isn't fun. You totally lied.

EMMY: Oh come on. I left out one little detail.

CLAIRE: Yeah. The pimping detail.   It's not exactly little.

EMMY: What did you think we were gonna do, Claire? Just stand there like awkward sophomores?

CLAIRE: We are awkward sophomores.

EMMY: I am not awkward.

CLAIRE: I thought we were gonna meet boys. Together. And then, I don't know, go home and laugh at how stupid they were for believing we were 21.

EMMY: We are gonna do that. That's exactly what we're gonna do. We're meeting my boy from last week. Plus his friend.

CLAIRE: I can't believe this.

EMMY: Oh come on.

CLAIRE: Emmy, you said you wanted to hang out.

EMMY: This is hanging out.

CLAIRE: No this is you sucking face with some guy and me getting stuck with the ugly friend.

(Claire gets up and moves over to the bed.)

EMMY: You should be flattered.

CLAIRE: Flattered?

EMMY: That I had so much faith in you. He told me to bring someone great, Claire. Someone smart and cute and great. And I picked you. Isn't that flattering?

CLAIRE: *(giving a little)*
You told him I'm cute?

EMMY: Yeah.

CLAIRE: And you said I'm smart?

EMMY: I said you're wicked smart.

(Claire smiles a little.)
But if you don't want to come...

CLAIRE: I'm coming.

EMMY: Just tell me now so I don't waste my artistry.

CLAIRE: I said I'm coming.

EMMY: All right.
(Emmy passes the wine bottle to Claire.)
It gets less scary the more you drink.
(Claire takes a sip.)
Let's pick your major.

CLAIRE: Well, you already created the fake me. You tell me what my fake major is.

EMMY: I told them you're a science major.

CLAIRE: There is no science major. It has to be a kind of science.

EMMY: Life science?

CLAIRE: You know, you're not as good at this as you think.

EMMY: Or Chemistry. Say Chemistry.

CLAIRE: I'm failing Chemistry.

EMMY: Well, it's not like there's gonna be a quiz. It's just a game, Claire. You act like you belong, and you belong.

CLAIRE: And if they don't believe me?

EMMY: Trust me, they won't exactly be looking for flaws.

(Emmy holds out a tissue to Claire.)

Blot.

(Claire blots her lipstick.)

And a little gloss for shine... And you're done.

(Emmy turns Claire to face the mirror.)

You like it?

CLAIRE: I don't even recognize myself.

EMMY: You're totally getting in.

CLAIRE: I am, aren't I?

(Claire examines herself in the mirror.)

Emmy, what did you do?

EMMY: Excuse me?

CLAIRE: With your guy. Last time.

EMMY: Claire.

CLAIRE: Well, I just- I was wondering.

EMMY: This is stupid.

CLAIRE: Second base? Third?

EMMY: You need to stop saying "bases." This isn't Camp Chicopee.

CLAIRE: Emmy--

EMMY: It doesn't matter. We did stuff. Just stuff among consenting adults. I don't feel the need to brag about it.

CLAIRE: Oh.

EMMY: Besides I was barely alone with him anyway. My sister is such an annoying Mom about that stuff.

CLAIRE: So you didn't...

EMMY: No.

CLAIRE: It's just- when you were dating Brian...

EMMY: When I was dating Brian, what?

CLAIRE: I just, I know you guys...

(She stops herself)

EMMY: ... Brian likes to talk.

CLAIRE: No, I... No one said anything to me.

(Emmy just looks at her.)

OK, I might've heard something, but...

EMMY: I don't care.

CLAIRE: So you guys did...

EMMY: Yeah.

CLAIRE: Oh.

EMMY: Twice.

CLAIRE: Wow.

EMMY: It's no big deal.

CLAIRE: Really? And you... Knew how to do it?

EMMY: My dog knows how to do it.

CLAIRE: Right, I know. It's just... When you think about what it actually is, it seems... Awkward.

EMMY: Well, I guess it could be. If you weren't... Ready, you know? If you weren't mature enough for it. But it wasn't awkward for me.

CLAIRE: Oh.

EMMY: It was perfect. You know? Just like it's supposed to be.
   (Pause)

CLAIRE: But tonight we're gonna... I mean, I'm just supposed to...
   (Emmy shrugs.)

EMMY: You're supposed to keep up.
   (Emmy reaches for a brush and begins to apply her own make-up. Claire settles in next to her to watch.)

Lascivious Something

Sheila Callaghan

Dramatic
Daphne, 23
Liza, mid to late-30s

Daphne, a beautiful Greek woman, lives on a small secluded island in the Ionian Sea with her much older ex-pat American husband August. Out of nowhere Liza, an old love of August's, shows up. She has an unnamed agenda. Here, on the evening of the first day of the visit, Daphne attempts to get at the heart of that agenda.

DAPHNE: Kali spera. *(Good evening.)* Have you eaten enough?

LIZA: Um yeah. Enough for a week...

DAPHNE: I am sorry you did not come on our walk with us. The sun setting onto the hill is poli orea. Very beautiful.

LIZA: Sunset, Christ... we were eating three hours straight...

DAPHNE: Yes. We do this. Lengthy eating. It is fortunate I enjoy to cook. It calms me. Did you know in Greece we have eighty-six ways to say "stop feeding me?"

LIZA: Why does that not surprise me.

DAPHNE: I do not understand the question.

LIZA: No, it. I meant. That it doesn't surprise me.

DAPHNE: Are you not easily surprised?

LIZA: Actually. Everything surprises me.

DAPHNE: Do I surprise you?

LIZA: In what way?

DAPHNE: When you first appeared you said I was beautiful, and then you said you were not prepared. This reveals you had an expectation. "The wife of Avgusto will be unattractive."

(Liza laughs.)

DAPHNE: *(cont.)*
You laugh because it rings of truth.

LIZA: Well I suppose I "expected" him to be with a woman who was alive when Kennedy was shot.

DAPHNE: I was alive. I was seven.

LIZA: Right.

DAPHNE: Does the age difference affect you?

LIZA: I was kidding / around

DAPHNE: American women are threatened by age. Why is this?

LIZA: Well, I don't know too many American women, so.

DAPHNE: No, I suppose you are uncommon. Avgusto would not care for a common woman.

(Daphne smiles hugely.)

You see how I compliment you and turn it back around to me? That is a cultural thing. French, I mean. I identify often with the French. Greek women tend to be more. There is an English word that means "under the service of men"...

LIZA: And you aren't?

DAPHNE: Of course I am. But it is different when the man is equally under the service of the woman. Yes?

LIZA: Ah.

(A beat.) (Liza peers around.)

So is, is he...

DAPHNE: He will be up shortly. He said he has getting something special. Is.

LIZA: Not dessert I hope.

DAPHNE: He did not say.

(An awkward silence.)

Tell me about where you live.

LIZA: I'd rather not.

DAPHNE: Why?

LIZA: I'm in transition.

DAPHNE: Surely you have a place to hang your clothing.

LIZA: I don't own a tremendous amount of clothing.

DAPHNE: You are being coy.

LIZA: No. I had, I DID have an apartment. In a building.

DAPHNE: A tall building? A "sky.." a sky/

LIZA: Not really. It, um. Six stories. Old carpet. The elevator is always broken. A radiator, um, you know don't take this the wrong way? I am not. Good at this. Aimless chatter. I kind of hate it.

DAPHNE: You are doing beautifully.

LIZA: I kind of really hate it.

(A beat.)

And now, you're. Um LOOKING at me, so, and I, I already talked about the food, and the view, the sunset, and I don't really want to talk about August, so.

Is there more wine?

DAPHNE: Liza, I feel I must be frank to you. I do not trust you. BUT, it is one of the reasons I feel so compelled by you.

LIZA: Oh.

DAPHNE: And you both speak very fast around one another, which also makes me feel strange.

LIZA: It's chilly, isn't it?

DAPHNE: We are without friends here and I feel grateful for your company and therefore I feel generous toward you. I wonder if you would like Boy to help you with anything.

LIZA: No. Should she be/ drink

DAPHNE: He is fine.

LIZA: Can she, okay, he speak English?

DAPHNE: Only how are you and have a nice day.

LIZA: He, actually she. Before, when I was sleeping.

DAPHNE: Yes. He likes to massage sometimes. Do not let it offend you. I wonder if it felt nice, though.

LIZA: Um.

DAPHNE: It is meant to relax you.

LIZA: Oh.

DAPHNE: I will mention to him not to do it again. But let us continue to talk frankly. I would like you to tell me something. With being frank.

LIZA: With being frank. Okay.

DAPHNE: Why are you here.

LIZA: That's a great question, Daphne. I'll answer it. Sure, no problem. I'll answer your question. I have no problem answering that question.
They stare each other down for several moments. It should be so long it looks as though both actors have forgotten their lines. REALLY long. No shorter than twenty seconds.

DAPHNE: But let us continue to talk frankly. I would like you to tell me something. With being frank.

LIZA: With being frank. Okay.

DAPHNE: Why are you here.

LIZA: I have something belonging to August that I need to return.
(A long beat.) (Daphne smiles.)

DAPHNE: I love the American sense of humor.
(Liza stares blankly at her.)

Love Letters Made Easy

Jeanne Beckwith

Seriocomic
Alice and Maureen, teens

> *Alice and Maureen are cleaning out Alice's maternal grandmother's house following Grandma's death. They find a box containing Grandma's love letters.*

ALICE: Incredible!

MAUREEN: My God! How many are there?

ALICE: Thirty, maybe? At least thirty.

MAUREEN: All that paper!

ALICE: All that ink!

MAUREEN: It must have taken hours to write them.

ALICE: When did he find the time? When did she?

MAUREEN: Why didn't she get rid of them?

ALICE: I don't know. Maybe it was too hard. It wouldn't be like deleting an e-mail. You'd actually have to tear them up one by one—or burn them in a pile. That's a lot of work.

MAUREEN: Maybe she just wanted to hang on to them until the last minute.

ALICE: Why?

MAUREEN: Why? Why do you think? They're hot.

ALICE: Maureen, you are talking about my 89-year old grandmother!

MAUREEN: There is some serious lust going on here. I think it's kinda cool.

ALICE: Cool? My 89-year old grandmother was cool?

MAUREEN: I'd say so. Apparently she was having a love affair up until practically the day she died. I'd say that was pretty cool.

ALICE: It was not very cool to leave all the evidence behind.

MAUREEN: No, but she probably intended to get rid of them and then death sneaked up on her.

ALICE: She was 89! She must have suspected it was a possibility.

MAUREEN: Maybe death always just kind of sneaks up on us.

ALICE: You think she loved this guy?

MAUREEN: He wrote an incredible letter.

ALICE: He did, didn't he?

MAUREEN: Some of these are recent. You think he's still alive?

ALICE: Why? You gonna look him up?

MAUREEN: I might think about it.

ALICE: You're sick.

MAUREEN: Well, your grandmother doesn't need him any more. I think it's sad to let something like this go to waste.

ALICE: Do you think he was at the funeral?

MAUREEN: There were a lot of geezers there. It could be.

ALICE: "Geezer Lust." Sounds like a song title.

MAUREEN: Well, this old bird could certainly sing. Look at this bit about the porch swing.

ALICE: How could anyone even do it in a porch swing?

MAUREEN: Maybe your grandfather wrote them. He just signs them "Syd." What was your grandfather's name? Would you recognize his handwriting?

ALICE: These are nothing my grandfather ever wrote. I remember my grandfather very well. His name was Martin, and anyway, he would never have—well, he just wouldn't have—not in a porch swing.

MAUREEN: Maybe not, but he's been dead a long time. She's been single since I've known you.

ALICE: She was not single. She was a widow. There's a difference.

MAUREEN: I don't know. Widows have a lot of time on their hands.

ALICE: My mother will crap when she reads these.

MAUREEN: You're going to show them to your mother?

ALICE: Well, I have to, don't I? Technically they're hers.

MAUREEN: You don't have to. Not if it would upset her. Nobody needs an upset Mom.

ALICE: Maybe I should just get rid of them.

MAUREEN: You should.

ALICE: You're right. I am most definitely getting rid of them

A Sleeping Country

Melanie Marnich

Julia, 20s-30
Midge, 30s

> *Julia has terrible insomnia and has come to Midge, a psychiatrist, for treatment.*
> *Julia and Dr. Midge in Dr. Midge's office. Julia has the manic energy that comes with exhaustion. Midge is bored.*

JULIA: I swear, I counted so many sheep there were flocks. Flocks of sheep. Then came the sheepherders. Then the sheepherding dogs. All over the place. Then I had to deal with that. It was awful. Tortuous. The night is infinite when you can't sleep, Midge. Not eight hours. Infinite. I wonder what Einstein's Theory of, of, of-

MIDGE: Relativity.

JULIA: What would Einstein have to say about that. It's the weirdest thing, Midge. Being so tired, feeling like everything is in place to fall asleep except for...sleep. Every night, the same thing. I start to feel tired around eleven, eleven-thirty. Brush my teeth, wash my face-

MIDGE *(pulling out a pocket tape recorder)* Reschedule racquetball.

JULIA: -snuggle in next to Greg, and just when I feel like I'm about to nod off...bam! Sleep's gone. Kaput. How can someone live like this is what I want to know. Because it's bone-breaking. This complete lack of, of, of relief. There are worse things to have, I'll grant you that. I read the papers. People are screwed out there. But this. I mean, how long can a body endure? Because I give, okay? I give!

MIDGE: Hearing you talk. Makes me think.

JULIA: An idea? What?

MIDGE: A question.

JULIA: About?

MIDGE: This whole engagement thing...

JULIA: Mine?

MIDGE: God no. Mine.

JULIA: You want to talk about you?

MIDGE: If you don't mind.

JULIA: Yeah, actually, I do.

MIDGE: I mean, what do you think about it?

JULIA: I think I want to talk about what I'm paying you to talk about.

MIDGE: We've been talking about your insomnia for months to no avail. It's getting monotonous.

JULIA: Not to me. To me it's getting urgent.

MIDGE: Seriously. What do you think about it?

JULIA: About?

MIDGE: The engagement. Being engaged. The state of being affianced.

JULIA: As it applies to you?

MIDGE: We can include you, since you're also engaged. But that's not as interesting to me. Sorry.

JULIA: You're unbelievable.

MIDGE: Indulge me.

JULIA: If we talk about you, can we eventually get back to me?

MIDGE *(checking her watch)*

Sure. But you'll have to make it snappy. I have a meditation class in an hour, so...

JULIA: You? Meditation?

MIDGE: Vipassana meditation. You sit on your ass and watch your thoughts. Shoot me. Shoot me now. Continue.

JULIA: Okay, well, personally, I like being engaged.

MIDGE: But you haven't taken it to "N."

JULIA: "N?"

MIDGE: "N." As in "nuptials."

JULIA: Not with Greg. But don't forget my first husband.

MIDGE: I always forget your first husband. You should try it. It feels great.

JULIA: Midge.

MIDGE: For fuck's sake, Julia, he designed dog toys.

JULIA: Organic dog toys. He's huge in Berkeley.

MIDGE: Who cares? Hemp is huge in Berkeley.

JULIA: Maintaining a train of thought with you is like- it's like my brain's an Etch-A-Sketch that someone keeps shaking.

MIDGE *(psychoanalyzing):*

Ahhh... So you're the Etch-A-Sketch and I'm the Shaker of the Etch-A-Sketch?

JULIA: Yeah.

MIDGE *(scribbling the note)*

I like that. Etch-a-whatever. Revealing. You were saying...?

JULIA: I think it's more like you were saying.

MIDGE: Parenthetically and FYI, "Vipassana" means "to see things as they really are." That sound like bullshit to you?

JULIA: No.

MIDGE: You were saying.

JULIA: I have no idea.

MIDGE *(prompting)*: You like being engaged...

JULIA: Oh. Right. Yeah. I love being engaged. I look forward to "N." However, and I say this with the utmost respect as someone who loves you like a sister, I don't think "N" is for you. You're just not "N" material. I mean, you're kind of a whore.

(A sigh from Midge.)

JULIA: What?

MIDGE: Oh, I dunno. "Not 'N' material." That's really personal and mean. So I need to clarify something. Psychiatry is about hurting the patient—not the psychiatrist. Let's get back on task.

JULIA: Sorry. I'm just... pissed off.

MIDGE: Why? You have a great fiancé.

JULIA: He's amazing.

MIDGE: A bright and beautiful future ahead of you both.

JULIA: Yeah.

MIDGE: And yet you're pissed. Why?

JULIA: At the moment, it's because I'm suffering from mind-numbing insomnia and you won't talk about it.

MIDGE: No excuse to attack my character like you did.

JULIA: I apologized. And I said I love you like a sister.

MIDGE: But you're only here because I see you at half my hourly rate. And because all the other shrinks gave up.

JULIA: And because you're a genius. You have three degrees from two Ivy League schools, a photographic memory and an IQ of one sixty-eight.

MIDGE: True. I am a bit of a diagnostic wunderkind. Just yesterday I correctly diagnosed this guy with Morgellons Disease. He'd been misdiagnosed with "delusional parasitosis" by some quack at Beth Israel. Anywho, back to your anxiety.

JULIA: I don't have anxiety.

MIDGE: Oh, I think you do.

JULIA: I really don't.

MIDGE: Think about it.

JULIA: Midge.

MIDGE: Fine, I'll think for you. You just got engaged. That's a big decision.

JULIA: Yes, it is.

MIDGE: It's a commitment.

JULIA: It is.

MIDGE: But "commitment" is a word with a lot of interpretations, a lot of variations, many shades of gray.

JULIA: Not really. That's why it's called "commitment."

MIDGE: For you, the word means...

JULIA: Commitment.

MIDGE: But for me, the more complicated of the two people in the room, it's more nuanced. Two people. Two different interpretations. Thus it is proven.

JULIA: What is proven is that you're a philanderer whose genitals should have their own driver's license. That's what is proven.

MIDGE: So what you're saying about me is...?

JULIA: Your heart may belong to one man, but your vagina belongs to the world.

MIDGE: I'm hearing you judging me.

JULIA: You're hearing me say you're a busy person. Not a bad person.

MIDGE: So you're implying...

JULIA: Do yourself a favor. Do Sven a favor.

MIDGE: Cedric. Sven was two mistakes ago. Cedric is a Buddhist. Thus this meditation crap.

JULIA: Don't get married. Trust me. It's easier to break up now before you have to get divorced.

MIDGE: Au contraire, my emotionally limited and groinally conservative pal. When you get divorced, at least you can hire lawyers to do the dirty work. If you're just dating, you have to do all the emotional heavy lifting yourself. Doesn't that seem wrong?

JULIA: No, it seems right and decent and like the very least you can do if-

MIDGE: Changing gears... How's work? Maybe the pressure's killing you. You're a graphic designer. Maybe advances in typography are getting to you.

JULIA: Not really.

MIDGE: Greg still write for that soap opera, "One Wife to Whatever?"

JULIA: "Life." "One Life to Embrace." Yeah, he does.

MIDGE: That's a cool job. Maybe you find his success emasculating?

JULIA: I'm a woman. How could I?

MIDGE: I would. So. This insomnia remains...

JULIA: Like an unspecific, vague cloudbank of panic deep in my gut.

MIDGE: About...? Come on, work with me, don't think too hard. About...?
(Julia thinks. Hard.)

JULIA: About...

MIDGE: About...?

JULIA: About…insomnia.

MIDGE: You are so tragically linear.
  (opening her file on Julia and reading):
  Moving on… Pharmaceutically speaking, we tried Trazadone…

JULIA: Didn't work.

MIDGE: Remeron…

JULIA: Nothing.

MIDGE: Temazepam, Xanax, Nebutol?

JULIA: No affect whatsoever.

MIDGE: Lunesta…

JULIA: Sucked.

MIDGE: Rozerem…

JULIA: Lame.

MIDGE: Sonata…

JULIA: Lamer.

MIDGE: Gaboxadol…

JULIA: Didn't work.

MIDGE: Estorra…

JULIA: Didn't work and made me hallucinate.

MIDGE: All the Ambiens… Yum.

JULIA: Didn't work and gave me amnesia.

MIDGE: Sweet. Melatonin… Valerian… Valium…

JULIA: Didn't work.

MIDGE: Nyquil? Tylenol P.M.?

JULIA: Useless.

MIDGE: Have you tried exceeding the recommended dosage?

JULIA: Always.

MIDGE: Did you ever use alcohol to intensify the affects of these drugs?

JULIA: Of course.

MIDGE: Atta girl. Maybe we should move on to antidepressants. Because insomnia can also be an indicator of depression.

JULIA: I'm not depressed.

MIDGE: Then you're in the minority. Most of America is clinically depressed, and it's the job of the mental health profession to make sure they're all medicated. Pill 'em. Pill 'em all. That's what we're trained to do.
  (Julia starts to cry.)

MIDGE: Oh. Oh. Honey.
  (Midge goes to her, holds her.)

JULIA *(crying)*: I'm so tired.
  (Then Midge starts to cry.)

MIDGE *(crying)*; I'm so bored.

JULIA *(crying)*:

> Then why are you crying?

MIDGE *(crying)*:

> It's just a reflex. Like when you see someone throw up and it makes you throw up. It doesn't mean anything.

JULIA *(crying)*:

> That's so sweet.

MIDGE *(crying)*:

> Don't tell anyone I do this, okay? It would damage my reputation as drunk, whoring genius.

JULIA *(crying)*:

> You care. I know you care. Thank you. I love you, Midge.

MIDGE *(stopping crying)*:

> I love you, too. But you have to scram. I have to meet Cedric at the temple of Rinpoche Whatshisname. Sorry.

JULIA: It's okay.

> *(They separate.)*

MIDGE: We'll figure this out, honey. It doesn't seem like it. But we will.

JULIA: You think so? Because I'm losing it, Midge. I'm really, really losing it.

MIDGE: I'm not gonna let you down, Jules. I'm officially on a medical mission. I promise.

JULIA: Really?

MIDGE: On my mother's grave.

JULIA: But she's still ali-

MIDGE: It's gonna be okay. Okay?

JULIA: *(walking away, waving goodbye)* Okay. Bye.

MIDGE: *(walking away, waving goodbye)* Bye bye.

Still Life

Alexander Dinelaris

Dramatic
Carrie Ann, 30s. A renowned photographer
Joanne, 30-50. Dean of a prestigious art school, she used to date Carrie Ann's
father.

*Carrie Ann, whose father has recently passed away, is offered an important
and glamorous job shooting photographs for National Geographic. However,
her boyfriend Jeff has just revealed to her that he has cancer. Joanne makes a
case as to why Carrie Ann should take the job and leave for a while.*

*(Joanne's office. Joanne sits, going through some work at her desk. After a bit,
Carrie Ann enters carrying a folder.)*

CARRIE ANN: Hey.

JOANNE: You're here late.

CARRIE ANN: I had some stuff I had to sort out. I'm going. I just wanted you
to see this.

She places the folder on Joanne's desk.

JOANNE: What is it?

CARRIE ANN: Jesse's new stuff. Take a look when you get a chance.

JOANNE: I've already seen them.

CARRIE ANN: What do you think?

JOANNE: I think they're young.

CARRIE ANN: They're young?

JOANNE: Yeah.

CARRIE ANN: What do you mean?

JOANNE: You know what I mean.

CARRIE ANN: I really don't.

(A beat.)

I got an interesting call today.

CARRIE ANN: Okay.

JOANNE: David Lucas from National Geographic called and told me they
want to send you to the Serengeti to shoot.

CARRIE ANN: Yeah.

JOANNE: You weren't going to tell me?

CARRIE ANN: No.

JOANNE: May I ask why?

CARRIE ANN: Because I'm not going.

JOANNE: Just like that?

CARRIE ANN: Just like that.

JOANNE: Okay. *(A beat.)* Now, is that because of your boyfriend or your father?

CARRIE ANN: Don't push me.

JOANNE: I think you should go.

CARRIE ANN: You know I can't.

JOANNE: Because your boyfriend's not well.

CARRIE ANN: His name is Jeff.

JOANNE: Because Jeff is not well. But neither are you, right? What about you?

CARRIE ANN: What's your point?

JOANNE: My point, baby, is that this is a big deal. Nat Geo in Tanzania is a big deal. On top of that, it's exactly what you need right now.

CARRIE ANN: And what? You expect me to leave him here?

JOANNE: I don't know. Take him with you.

CARRIE ANN: Sure. Cause there are a lot of great treatment centers in the Serengeti.

JOANNE: Come back every other week. Explain the situation to them. I'm sure they'll understand. What's it gonna add, two or three weeks to the shoot? They want you. It won't make a difference, and you know it.

CARRIE ANN: I didn't come here to talk about this. I'm going home.

(Carrie Ann turns to leave.)

JOANNE: Your father wasn't such a great photographer.

CARRIE ANN: *(She turns back.)*

Why would you say that to me?

JOANNE: Because you need to hear it. He wasn't. We both know that. But you are. You're great. Tough shit. Deal with it. Look, I can't imagine what those last few months were like for you. But its over. You're still here. Except now you meet this guy, and he gets sick, too. That's just-- I don't know. That's either horrible fucking luck, or you're radioactive. I don't know. *(A beat.)* Maybe you're right. Maybe the world is coming to an end. But what are you gonna do in the meantime?

(A pause.)

What?

CARRIE ANN: How would you know he wasn't good? Who are you to say? You have no idea what you're talking about. "It's young?" You slobber over these kids' work and infect their vision, until all their shots look like the shots you would've taken if you had any talent yourself. Twenty years ago you liked his work just fine. Until those influential friends of yours told you he wasn't sophisticated enough. So you dumped him. And you grabbed onto me. *(A beat.)* It destroyed him, Jo. He wouldn't admit it, but it did. It destroyed us. All those times when we would just sit there and laugh and talk about each other's work turned into these sickening seven word conversations. "How's your stuff?" "Are they gonna show it?" Good for you baby, you deserve it." Every show, every award, drove us that much further apart. But you didn't bother to notice, cause you got what you wanted, didn't you?

(A beat.)

JOANNE: You feel better?

CARRIE ANN: Excuse me?

JOANNE: Yeah. I mean, you've been waiting a long time to deliver that speech. I was wondering if you feel better now.

CARRIE ANN: Fuck you.

JOANNE: You want to attack me? Fine. There are a lot of things I deserve it for. But not for telling you the truth. Go. Don't go. Do whatever the hell you want. But don't blame me. *(A beat.)* Like it or not, you have to start taking pictures again. You have to start living again. Because the alternative is just more death. *(A beat.)* There's still life out there, Carrie Ann. What are you gonna do with it?

A Thing for Redheads

John Morogiello

Comic
Bobbie O'Connor, 40 (in the play, a redhead)
Jessie MORGAN, 19 (in the play, a redhead)

Bobbie, an emotionally distraught Pulitzer Prize-winning author, has spent the past three years working on her follow-up novel and has fallen in love with Peter, her womanizing editor. Peter prefers Jessie, a teenage singer whose autobiography he has been asked to ghost-write. Stanley, Peter's unattractive brother and business partner, doesn't like that Bobbie is being dumped for Jessie and has begun to carry a baseball bat around the office to threaten Peter. Here, she has it out with Jessie.

(Bobbie turns away from Peter's door as Jessie enters from the main door. Small beat as they size each other up. Jessie chooses to be friendly.)

JESSIE: Hi.

BOBBIE: Peter's busy at the moment. Why don't you have a seat.

JESSIE: You're the receptionist? I thought you were, like, a writer?

BOBBIE: Only like a writer. I haven't been the real thing for three years.

JESSIE: Have you talked to Peter? He can, like, write it for you? And you just put your name on it!

BOBBIE: Is that so.

JESSIE: That's how I'm writing my book. It's kind of like being in high school again. Only Peter's not a nerd. Okay, like, usually? When it comes to writing? I'd go with a nerd every time. It's a quality thing. But did you see the nerd on staff? I was, like, totally freaked. Plus Peter's just got this thing going, you know? OMG! The way he looks at you and, like, holds your hand: you can tell he's real smart.

BOBBIE: *(Elsewhere.)*
Yeah.

JESSIE: I'm hoping we can knock this book thing out in a couple of days. I had to, like, totally mess with my recording schedule. Pissed off a bunch of people with cash.

BOBBIE: Whole book in a couple of days.

JESSIE: They can do that, right? It's not like its gotta be Shakespeare or Hamlet or Harry Potter or anything.

BOBBIE: Can I give you some advice?

JESSIE: What.

BOBBIE: Go. Get out of here and don't look back.

JESSIE: What?

BOBBIE: Find someone else to write it for you.

JESSIE: Like, why?

BOBBIE: Peter's dangerous.

JESSIE: In what way?

BOBBIE: He's got a thing for redheads.

JESSIE: ...I know. ...Thanks. --Mine's natural.

BOBBIE: --Everything of mine is natural.

JESSIE: I can tell. ...Well, thanks for the advice. Maybe I can use it.

BOBBIE: --Use it?

JESSIE: To my advantage.

BOBBIE: He's a grown man. You're just a kid.

JESSIE: Yeah, but I'm not, like, some naive thing. I know I act like it sometimes, but I view stupid as a means to an end. You know what I'm saying? You do it, right? We all do. I've been in this business for two whole years. And after awhile, you learn to be a little cutthroat.

BOBBIE: I'm trying to give you a warning.

JESSIE: About what?

BOBBIE: About not ending up like me.

(Beat.) (Jessie chooses to be polite again.)

JESSIE: Thank you. --Somehow I don't think that will be a problem for many years.

BOBBIE: He's seeing someone.

JESSIE: Yeah?

BOBBIE: Longer than you've been in the business.

(Jessie looks at Bobbie up and down and suppresses a laugh.)

JESSIE: Oh.

BOBBIE: Why are you laughing?

JESSIE: Well... Are, like, you the competition? ...I win!

BOBBIE: I know what Peter likes.

JESSIE: I am what Peter likes.

BOBBIE: With my experience? You don't stand a chance.

JESSIE: Against some old-lady writer? Please! I'm a singer. Guys don't want to read stuff and think; they want to relax and watch.

BOBBIE: You don't watch a singer! You watch a pole-dancer.

JESSIE: You mighta been hot once, but you're, like, so past now, it's not even funny. Face it, I'm every man's dream: I got the pipes, I got the body, and I got a brain he can feel smart around.

(Pause.) (Bobbie betrays her insecurity.)
BOBBIE: You're lucky Stanley took the bat.

Trust

Paul Weitz

Seriocomic
Prudence, late 20s
Aleeza, late 20s

> *Prudence is a dominatrix. Aleeza, who has just left her husband, has
> wondered into her dungeon. At first, she asks for a session, but it soon becomes
> clear that she thinks becoming a dominatrix might be something she could
> do to support herself.*

*(Lights up on Prudence's room at the S and M parlor. Aleeza comes in.
Aleeza looks around the room. Looks at the handcuffs. Prudence comes out.)*

ALEEZA: Hello.

PRUDENCE: *(pause)*

Hi.

ALEEZA: *(holds up Prudence's card)* Thought I'd drop by after all.

She puts the card on the chair.

PRUDENCE: What do you want?

ALEEZA: ...A tour?

(pause)

So what's in the other rooms? Are they just like this one?

PRUDENCE: *(pause)*

No. There are different types. There's one room with a lot of cages. There's
one room with a dentist's chair. There's a medieval torture room.

ALEEZA: So this one is pretty no frills.

PRUDENCE: Yeah. This is submission 101.

ALEEZA: Do you only work in this room?

PRUDENCE: ...No, I've worked in the other ones.

ALEEZA: How much do you get paid? I mean, I know it's 150 an hour, plus tip.
But how much of that do you get?

PRUDENCE: I don't talk about that.

ALEEZA: Come on, I won't tell anyone. What is it?

PRUDENCE: ...Eighty-three dollars and forty-nine cents. Plus tip. Tip can be
anything from ten to a few hundred dollars.

ALEEZA: Seriously?

PRUDENCE: Seriously.

(pause)

Anything else?

ALEEZA: I left my husband.

PRUDENCE: *(pause)*

You left him?

ALEEZA: I've moved out. Yes.

(pause)

So I'd like to do a session.

PRUDENCE: ...You don't want to do a session with me.

ALEEZA: Why not?

PRUDENCE: Because it's my last day here.

ALEEZA: Oh.

PRUDENCE: Doing just one session is useless. You need someone you can develop a rapport with. It's about trust.

ALEEZA: Trust?

PRUDENCE: Yeah. Somewhere in the back of your head you have to know that you're not going to get really hurt.

ALEEZA: Doesn't that take the fun out of it?

PRUDENCE: It's not about fun.

ALEEZA: What's it about?

PRUDENCE: Accepting yourself. Even if it's temporary...

ALEEZA: So what are you gonna do?

PRUDENCE: I don't know.

(pause)

I have no idea. Anyway, I can recommend someone else for you.

ALEEZA: I don't really want a session with someone else. In fact, I don't really want a session.

PRUDENCE: What do you want?

ALEEZA: I want a job. I want to do what you do for a living. I want you to teach me how to do it...

(nods)

Please, teach me.

PRUDENCE: It's not what you think. Whatever you think this is going to be like. It's not like that. Working here. Whatever you want to learn about yourself. You can't really learn it. It's like trying to grab your reflection in a pool of water.

ALEEZA: Maybe...Maybe just for you. Maybe not for me. *(pause)*

I thought I could trail you.

PRUDENCE: "Trail me?" This isn't a waitressing job.

ALEEZA: Then how do you learn?

PRUDENCE: ...You trail someone.

ALEEZA: Please. I need to do this.

PRUDENCE: Why?

ALEEZA: I don't know why. I just know I need it.

> *(pause)*

PRUDENCE: What was your father like?

ALEEZA: My father? ...Six foot three.

PRUDENCE: What was he like? Was he a loving father? Was he abusive?

ALEEZA: What does that have to do with anything? What was your father like?

PRUDENCE: He was a lawyer for the arch-diocese. A while after I hit puberty he stopped talking to me. I felt like I'd committed some kind of crime by getting my period and growing breasts. Then he died.

ALEEZA: ...When my parents got divorced, he told me he couldn't talk to my mother because she was too unintelligent. I was ten. *(shrugs)* How was that?

PRUDENCE: Okay. Did you hate him?

ALEEZA: No, I loved him.

PRUDENCE: Were you worried that he thought you were stupid too?

ALEEZA: No, I was worried that he *knew* I was stupid. Were you worried that your father wanted to fuck you?

PRUDENCE: No, he was too afraid of getting me pregnant.

> *(She stands there for a moment. Then she goes to the cart.)*

PRUDENCE: Alright. I use four different kinds of manacles. These are basic handcuffs. They hurt a little. Then there are these leather ones. They're more comfortable until they start to sweat, then they chafe. These...these ones are for beginners.

ALEEZA: Can I see?

> She goes to the cart.

ALEEZA: What are these?

PRUDENCE: Clamps. For the nipples, or the genitals. These little ones you can use on the scrotum. Or on a woman's vulva.

ALEEZA: ...Okay.

PRUDENCE: These are all just tools, though. The main thing's up here.

> *(Prudence points to her head)*

> Out there, in the outside world, there's a give and take. Sometimes you're in control of a situation, sometimes not.

ALEEZA: Usually not.

PRUDENCE: ...Usually not.

> *(pause)*

> But once the client walks through that door, *you* are in control. He's not. In here, this...

(points to her head)
Is in control of this...
(points to her heart)
Always.
ALEEZA: Sounds great.
PRUDENCE: Yeah, well...it's just a fantasy.

Rights and permissions

The entire text of each play may be obtained by contacting the rights holder.

Note: For playwrights whose names are followed by an asterisk (*), information can be found about them on the "Meet our authors" web page at www.smithandkraus.com

MONOLOGUES

AFTERLIFE: A GHOST STORY © 2009 by Steve Yockey. Reprinted by permission of Scott Edwards, Harden-Curtis Assoc. For performance rights, contact Scott Edwards (scottedwards@hardencurtis.com)

ALIVE AND WELL © 2009 by Kenny Finkle. Reprinted by permission of Beth Blickers, Abrams Artists Agency. For performance rights, contact Beth Blickers (beth.blickers@abramsartny.com)

ALL IN THE FACULTY © 2010 by William Fowkes *. Reprinted by permission of Richard Seff. For performance rights, contact Dramatists Play Service, 440 Park Ave. S., New York, NY 10016 (www.dramatists.com) (212-683-8960).

THE AWAKENING OF KATE CHOPIN © 2011 by Rosary O'Neill *. Reprinted by permission of Tonda Marton, The Marton Agency. For performance rights, contact Samuel French, Inc. (www.samuelfrench.com) (212-206-8990).

BIRTHDAY © 2011 by Crystal Skillman*. Reprinted by permission of Crystal Skillman. For performance rights, contact Samuel French, Inc. (www.samuelfrench.com) (212-206-8990).

THE BREAK OF NOON © 2010 by Neil LaBute. Reprinted by permission of Jodi Hammerwold, SoftSkull Press, c/o Counterpoint Press. For performance rights, contact Joyce Ketay, The Gersh Agency (jketay@gershny.com)

A BRIGHT NEW BOISE © 2010 by Samuel D. Hunter. Reprinted by permission of Derek Zasky, William Morris Endeavor Entertainment. For performance rights, contact Samuel French, Inc. (www.samuelfrench.com) (212-206-8990)

CLASS © 2010 by Charles Evered. Reprinted by permission of Susan Gurman, Susan Gurman Agency. For performance rights, contact Broadway Play Publishing, 56 E. 81st St., New York, NY 10021 (www.broadwayplaypubl.com) 212-772-8334.

CLYTEMNESTRA © 2010 by Don Nigro. Reprinted by permission of Don Nigro. For performance rights, contact Samuel French, Inc. (www.samuelfrench.com) (212-206-8990).

COLLAPSE © 2010 by Allison Moore. Reprinted by permission of Beth Blickers & Maura Teitelbaum, Abrams Artists Agency. For performance rights, contact Beth Blickers (beth.blickers@abramsartny.com)or Maura Teitelbaum (maura.teitelbaum@abramsartny.com)

A COMMON VISION © 2009 by Neena Beber*. Reprinted by permission of Mark Subias, Mark Subias Agency. For performance rights, contact Samuel French, Inc. (www.samuelfrench.com) (212-206-8990).

A CONFLUENCE OF DREAMING (2) © 2010 by Tammy Ryan.* Reprinted by permission of Susan Gurman, Susan Gurman Agency. For performance rights, contact Broadway Play Publishing, 56 E. 81st St., New York, NY 10021 (www.broadwayplaypubl.com) (212-772-8334.)

THE DEATH BITE © 2010 by Hal Corley. Reprinted by permission of Barbara Hogenson, Barbara Hogenson Agency. For performance rights, contact Barbara Hogenson (Bhogenson@aol.com)

THE DEW POINT © 2009 by Neena Beber*. Reprinted by permission of Mark Subias, Subias Agency. For performance rights, contact Samuel French, Inc. (www.samuelfrench.com) (212-206-8990).

THE DIVINE SISTER © 2010 by Charles Busch*. Reprinted by permission of Olivier Sultan, Creative Artists Agency. For performance rights, contact Samuel French, Inc. (www.samuelfrench.com) (212-206-8990).

DRAMATIS PERSONAE © 2007 by Gonzalo Rodriguez Risco*. Reprinted by permission of Gonzalo Rodriguez Risco. For performance rights, contact Gonzalo Rodriguez Risco (gonzalo.rodriguez@aya.yale.edu)

DUSK RINGS A BELL © 2010 by Stephen Belber*. Reprinted by permission of Stephen Belber. For performance rights, contact Dramatists Play Service, 440 Park Ave. S., New York, NY 10016 (www.dramatists.com) (212-683-8960).

EASTER MONDAY © 2009 by Hal Corley*. Reprinted by permission of Barbara Hogenson, Barbara Hogenson Agency. For performance rights, contact Samuel French, Inc. (www.samuelfrench.com) (212-206-8990).

FLOWER DUET © 2010 by Maura Campbell*. Reprinted by permission of Maura Campbell. For performance rights, contact Maura Campbell (ibsen3000@yahoo.com).

GHOSTS IN THE COTTONWOODS © 2010 by Adam Rapp*. Reprinted by permission of Mark Subias, Subias Agency. For performance rights, contact Mark Subias (mark@marksubias.com)

GIRLS IN TROUBLE © 2010 by Jonathan Reynolds*. Reprinted by permission of Jonathan Reynolds. For performance rights, contact Broadway Play Publishing, 56 E. 81st St., New York, NY 10021 (www.broadwayplaypubl.com) 212-772-8334.

GOODBYE NEW YORK, GOODBYE HEART © 2010 by Lally Katz*. Reprinted by permission of Jean Mostyn, The Yellow Agency. For performance rights, contact Lally Katz (lallykatz@gmail.com)

GRACE © 2010 by Craig Wright. Reprinted by permission of Beth Blickers, Abrams Artists Agency. For performance rights, contact Dramatists Play Service, 440 Park Ave. S., New York, NY 10016 (www.dramatists.com) (212-683-8960).

GRAND CAYMAN © 2009 by Don Nigro, Reprinted by permission of Don Nigro. For performance rights, contact Samuel French, Inc. (www.samuelfrench.com) (212-206-8990).

GRUESOME PLAYGROUND INJURIES © 2011 by Rajiv Joseph*. Reprinted by permission of Seth Glewen, The Gersh Agency. For performance rights, contact Dramatists Play Service, 440

Park Ave. S., New York, NY 10016 (www.dramatists.com) (212-683-8960). .

THE HOUSEWIVES OF MANNHEIM © 2010 by Alan Brody*. Reprinted by permission of Earl Graham, Graham Agency. For performance rights, contact Earl Graham (grahamacynyc@aol.com)

IN THE WAKE © 2010 by Lisa Kron. Reprinted by permission of Patrick Herold, International Creative Management. For performance rights, contact Dramatists Play Service, 440 Park Ave. S., New York, NY 10016 (www.dramatists.com) (212-683-8960). .

THE LANGUAGE ARCHIVE © 2010 by Julia Cho*. Reprinted by permission of John Buzzetti, William Morris Endeavor Entertainment. For performance rights, contact Dramatists Play Service, 440 Park Ave. S., New York, NY 10016 (www.dramatists.com) (212-683-8960).

LASCIVIOUS SOMETHING © 2011 by Savage Candy Productions f/s/o Sheila Callaghan* c/o The Gersh Agency. Reprinted by permission of Seth Glewen The Gersh Agency. For performance rights, contact Samuel French, Inc. (www.samuelfrench.com) (212-206-8990)

LEAVES © 2007 by Lucy Caldwell*. Reprinted by permission of Harriet Pennington Legh, Alan Brodie Representation Ltd. For performance rights, contact Dramatists Play Service, 440 Park Ave. S., New York, NY 10016 (www.dramatists.com) (212-683-8960).

LET'S NOT TALK ABOUT MEN © 2010 by Carla Cantrelle. Reprinted by permission of the author. Published by Smith and Kraus, Inc. in The Best 10-Minute Plays of 2011. For performance rights, contact Smith and Kraus, Inc. (www.smithandkraus.com).

LINER NOTES © 2010 by John Patrick Bray*. Reprinted by permission of John Patrick Bray. For performance rights, contact John Patrick Bray (johnpatrickbray@yahoo.com)

LOCAL NOBODY © 2009 by Nicole Pandolfo*. Reprinted by permission of Nicole Pandolfo. For performance rights, contact Nicole Pandolfo (nicole.e.pandolfo@gmail.com)

LOVE LETTERS MADE EASY © 2010 by Jeanne Beckwith*. Reprinted by permission of Jeanne Beckwith. For performance rights, contact Jeanne Beckwith (rialto@tds.net)

MARBLE © 2010 by Marina Carr. Reprinted by permission of Jean Barry, The Gallery Press. For performance rights, contact Dramatists Play Service, 440 Park Ave. S., New York, NY 10016 (www.dramatists.com) (212-683-8960).

THE METAL CHILDREN © 2010 by Adam Rapp*. Reprinted by permission of Mark Subias, Subias Agency. For performance rights, contact Mark Subias (mark@marksubias.com).

MIRACLE ON SOUTH DIVISION STREET © 2008 by Tom Dudzick*. Reprinted by permission of Jack Tantleff, Paradigm Agency. For performance rights, contact Jack Tantleff (jtantleff@paradigmagency.com)

MOTHERHOUSE © 2010 by Victor Lodato. Reprinted by permission of Beth Blickers & MORGAN Jenness, Abrams Artists Agency. For performance rights, contact Samuel French, Inc. (www.samuelfrench.com) (212-206-8990).

THE OTHER PLACE © 2009 by Sharr White*. Reprinted by permission of Peregrine Whittlesey, Peregrine Whittlesey Agency. For performance rights, contact Dramatists Play

AFTER THE REVOLUTION © 2010 by Amy Herzog*. Reprinted by permission of Val Day, William Morris Endeavor Entertainmant. For performance rights, contact Dramatists Play Service, 440 Park Ave. S., New York, NY 10016 (www.dramatists.com) (212-683-8960)

COLLAPSE © 2010 by Allison Moore. Reprinted by permission of Beth Blickers & Maura Teitelbaum, Abrams Artists Agency. For performance rights, contact Beth Blickers (beth. blickers@abramsartny.com) or Maura Teitelbaum (maura.teitelbaum@abramsartny.com)

THE DEW POINT © 2009 by Neena Beber*. Reprinted by permission of Mark Subias, Subias Agency. For performance rights, contact Samuel French, Inc. (www.samuelfrench.com) (212-206-8990)

ELEMENO PEA © 2011 by Molly Smith Metzler. Reprinted by permission of Kate Navin, Abrams Artists Agency. For performance rights, contact Kate Navin (kate.navin@abramsartny. com)

GOODBYE NEW YORK, GOODBYE HEART © 2010 by Lally Katz*. Reprinted by permission of Jean Mostyn, The Yellow Agency. For performance rights, contact Lally Katz (lallykatz@gmail.com)

THE HOUSEWIVES OF MANNHEIM © 2010 by Alan Brody*. Reprinted by permission of Earl Graham, Graham Agency. For performance rights, contact Earl Graham (grahamacynyc@ aol.com)

IN THE WAKE © 2010 by Lisa Kron. Reprinted by permission of Patrick Herold, International Creative Management. For performance rights, contact Dramatists Play Service, 440 Park Ave. S., New York, NY 10016 (www.dramatists.com) (212-683-8960).

JAILBAIT © 2010 by Deirdre O'Connor. Reprinted by permission of Jessica Amato, The Gersh Agency. For performance rights, contact Dramatists Play Service, 440 Park Ave. S., New York, NY 10016 (www.dramatists.com) (212-683-8960)

LASCIVIOUS SOMETHING © 2010 by Sheila Callaghan*. Reprinted by permission of Seth Glewen, The Gersh Agency. For performance rights, contact Samuel French, Inc. (www. samuelfrench.com) (212-206-8990)

LOVE LETTERS MADE EASY © 2010 by Jeanne Beckwith*. Reprinted by permission of Jeanne Beckwith. For performance rights, contact Jeanne Beckwith (rialto@tds.net)

A SLEEPING COUNTRY © 2010 by Melanie Marnich*. Reprinted by permission of Val Day, William Morris Endeavor Entertainmant. For performance rights, contact Dramatists Play Service, 440 Park Ave. S., New York, NY 10016 (www.dramatists.com) (212-683-8960).

STILL LIFE © 2010 by Alexander Dinaris*. Reprinted by permission of Olivier Sultan, Creative Artists Agency. For performance rights, contact Dramatists Play Service, 440 Park Ave. S., New York, NY 10016 (www.dramatists.com) (212-683-8960).

A THING FOR REDHEADS © 2008 by John Morogiello*. Reprinted by permission of John